AL CAPONE'S MIAMI
Paradise or Purgatory?

Date: 5/18/16

AL CAPONE'S MIAMI
Paradise or Purgatory?

SALLY J. LING

Published by Flamingo Press
Deerfield Beach, Florida 33442

Cover image by Terry Boorman

Cover design by Andy Massari

First published 2015

ISBN-13:978-0-9964333-1-0

TABLE OF CONTENTS

AKNOWLEDGEMENTS

I'd like to thank those individuals who generously provided their knowledge and assistance in helping me take *Al Capone's Miami: Paradise or Purgatory?* from concept to publication:

Sandi Altner, fellow author and friend, for her initial suggestion that I tackle this subject;

Stuart Hanley, Carol Orr Hartman, Dawn McMillan, Tom Orr, David Eller, and the Reverend Lee Pearson who shared stories and/or photos of family members who had personal encounters with Al Capone;

Kelly Brown, Reference Services Assistant Supervisor of the Broward County Library (North Region/BC), and Amy Miller, Interlibrary Loan Supervisor, Broward County Main Library, for their incredible knowledge and assistance with archived newspapers and book resources; Rebekah Tomlinson Mendoza for her genealogical research; Carolyn Klepser and Jeff Donn, historians, for their knowledge of Miami and Miami Beach; John Shipley, Head of the Florida Collection, Miami-Dade County Public Library System, for his assistance with resource materials; Dawn Hughes, History Miami, Liliam Hatfield, Assistant City Clerk City of Miami Beach, and Howard Lanza, Garfield Historical Society, for their assistance with images;

Lisa Dykstra and Rebekah Tomlinson Mendoza for their keen eyes;

Pat Keeley and Dr. Judith Lombana for their fine editing.

Photos contained in this book are courtesy of the author unless otherwise noted.

PREFACE

Most have heard of Alphonse "Al" Gabriel Capone, also known as "Scarface," who rose to become the undisputed king of the Chicago outfit during the Prohibition era. Most know he became one of America's most infamous gangsters who earned the moniker "Public Enemy Number One." His connection to New York and Chicago crime families, the running of gambling dens, whorehouses, and speakeasies, and reports of his committing assorted murders is legendary and readily acknowledged in myriad books, documentaries, and TV shows. But few know the intimate details about his time in Florida, especially the greater Miami area. It was here he hoped to escape Chicago's cold and windy winters, gangland retaliation wars, and incessant hounding by the law.

Capone longed for paradise, where sunshine was a daily commodity, boating and fishing could be easily enjoyed along a sandy coast lapped by azure Atlantic waters, nightlife teemed with high class entertainment clubs and gambling houses, and relaxing by the pool was as easy as stepping out your back door. And so, Capone settled in South Florida where he purchased a luxurious home on Miami Beach, spent time before and after his imprisonment, ran his illegal businesses, and entertained the famous and infamous alike. It is here he also died.

This story is about that time.

CHAPTER 1

THE MAKING OF A GANGSTER

Once you're in the racket, you're always in it.[1]
Al Capone

The wail of a red-faced newborn, a baby boy, announced the birth of another infant to Gabriel and Theresa Capone on January 17, 1899. The recent addition, christened Alphonse "Al" Gabriel Capone, was the fourth child born into the blue-collar household, but it wouldn't be their last. Four more children would eventually be welcomed into the growing family.

In 1893, Gabriel, 28 and a barber by trade, had emigrated from Italy to America along with his 23-year-old pregnant wife and their first two children.[2] Having arrived by steamer along with thousands of others from Europe, the couple was introduced to the land of opportunity through Ellis Island. There, they were documented and ushered into the bustling city of New York to begin their new life where an uncertain but hopeful future awaited.

The family first settled into a squalid tenement near the Brooklyn Navy Yard, a tough New York neighborhood where sailors frequented local bars and brothels then staggered through neglected streets. While the Capone's displayed the typical liveliness of Italian-American families, they were law-abiding citizens, and there were few hints that any of their children would enter a life of crime.

For the most part, Al's early years were uneventful, spending them cocooned in ethnically familiar surroundings. His teen years, however, took a turn for the worse when the family moved to the culturally diverse South Brooklyn community that exposed him to unsavory influences.[3]

Attendance at a Catholic school described as "inadequate and brutal . . . beset with violence,"[4] seemed to exacerbate Al's years in the new neighborhood where he learned to become a fast-thinking and hard-fighting young lad. Though he maintained a B average until the sixth grade, the lure of pool halls and sand lots eventually kept him from classes—hooky-playing days that accounted for 57 of 90 days in one school term.[5]

Al's first association with an organized ring came around the age of twelve when he joined the James Street Boys that engaged in burglaries, robberies, gambling, and loan-sharking. It was run by Johnny "The Fox" Torrio, 17 years his senior. But Lower Manhattan with the more powerful Five Points gang headed by Paul Kelly (Paulo Antonio Vaccarelli), loomed on the horizon. Kelly recruited Torrio who eventually became his second in command. Keeping a sharp eye out for tough young boys whom he could draft into his Five Points Junior gang, Torrio put Al at the top of his list.[6]

Young Capone remained in school until age fourteen when his fiery temper, well-known in the neighborhood, got the best of him. One day during a scolding by a female teacher he exploded, striking her. He was immediately sent to the principal's office where he received a whipping. After that, he left school and never returned.[7] Deirdre Marie Capone in her book *Uncle Al Capone* disputes this account however, insisting her Uncle Al graduated from high school.[8]

By sixteen, Capone had become an integral member of both the Five Points gang in Manhattan and a gang in Brooklyn headed by Torrio associate Frankie Yale whose main income was produced through classic racketeering.[9] Two years later, Yale employed Capone as bartender and bouncer at the Harvard Inn, a Brooklyn saloon and dance hall that he owned.[10] Capone became his rising understudy.

Torrio moved to Chicago in 1909 where he assisted in the running of "Big Jim" Colosimo's criminal empire that included gambling, racketeering, and hundreds of brothels. He also dealt with extortion demands from the rival "Black Hand" ring by eliminating them through his standard marksmanship.[11]

During this time, Capone, still in New York, was being mentored by Yale. It was there, one account states,[12] that he received the nickname "Scarface." It happened at the Harvard Inn when Capone insulted Lena Galluccio and was slashed with a knife—twice across the left cheek and once on the neck—by the girl's brother Frank. Yet, another version[13] noted he was sliced across the face with a razor by an "undersized, quick-tempered Sicilian" who, after being bullied, backed Capone into a corner in a Fourth Avenue barber shop. Either way, the scars and the name were Capone's for life.

On December 30, 1918, at age 19, Capone married Mae Josephine Coughlin, an Irish-Catholic girl. Just a few weeks earlier on December 4, 1918, Mae had given birth to the couple's son, Albert Francis "Sonny" Capone.[14] He would be their only child.

After Capone assaulted a rival gang member to the point of near death, Yale sent him to work with Torrio in Chicago until things cooled off. Capone arrived in the Windy City eager to accept his next assignment and later moved his family into a house at 7244 South Prairie Avenue.[15]

In 1920, Prohibition became the law of the land. This ushered in the windfall business of importing illegal booze and the serving of same in clandestine private clubs called speakeasies where a rap on the door, recognition through a peep hole, and secret password were keys to gaining entry. Torrio saw Prohibition as an enormous opportunity to magnify the gang's influence and gain great strides both financially and organizationally. But "Big Jim" Colosimo didn't see it that way. He refused to enter the bootlegging business believing it would draw unwelcome attention to his organization by police. Torrio regarded this decision as a greatly missed opportunity.

On May 11, Colosimo was gunned down in the main foyer of his own establishment, Colosimo's Cafe. Yale, Torrio's old pal from New York, was implicated as the hit man since he was in Chicago at the time, but no one was ever prosecuted. Torrio and Capone, who became known as the "Outfit," took over Colosimo's vast criminal empire and ventured into a new enterprise—rum running.[16] This would eventually lead Capone to the warm shores of Miami.

Rum Running and South Florida

In 1913, seven years before Prohibition became the law of the land, Dade County in southern Florida held a referendum to determine whether the county would stay wet or go dry. When the votes were tallied, the drys had won. The southern portion of the county—Miami—had voted to remain wet, while citizens in the northern part—Fort Lauderdale, Dania, and Hallandale—had voted to go dry. This stunned Miami residents. After struggling to overturn the election six times, citing the fact that these northern cities really resided in Broward County, a new county the 1913 legislature had already legally created, Miamians claimed the wets had actually won the election with a majority of the votes. The courts, however, didn't buy the argument, and Dade County turned dry . . . at least on paper.[17]

After the law became reality, illegal booze flowed into Miami from counties further north or the Bahamas just off Florida's east coast. Since Miami was in the middle of a land boom and the town depended upon tourists having "fun in the sun," law enforcement officials turned a blind eye to the acquisition and serving of the unlawful nectar. They also turned a blind eye to Miami's prohibited gambling that seemed to go hand in hand with the banished booze.

> *Casinos ran without pretense of concealment: slot machines whirred and jingled in nearly every store and hotel lobby, and police moonlighted as escorts delivering the slots' proceeds. On Miami Beach, the city manager, Claude A. Henshaw [sic], had the concession for giving operators approval.[18]*

In 1920 when Prohibition became the law of the land, supplies of booze from the north dried up, yet southern Floridians would not be denied. They turned their eyes, and pocketbooks, fully to the east.

Bahamas Becomes Booze Distribution Empire

Nassau, the capital of the Bahamas, became the business hub for representatives of liquor companies from Britain and Jamaica that imported distilled liquors, champagnes, and liqueurs into the British-controlled colony. Shingles dangling from offices on Bay and Market Streets in Nassau invited willing rumrunners to make arrangements with the shrewd distributors. Just outside town, huge 30- by 50-foot barges packed with crates of booze from off shore distilleries, floated on a sapphire bay.

Nassau, along with other accessible Bahamian settlements such as Bimini (forty-five miles from Miami) or West End on Grand Bahama Island (fifty-five miles from Palm Beach), became established distribution points. Other imports came from Cuba, ninety miles south of Key West. Thus, Cuba, the Bahamas, and the shores of South Florida were appropriately dubbed the "liquid gold triangle."[19] It was out of this geometric figure that illegal alcohol flowed freely into and through the southern Florida peninsula like water bursting from a levee.

Cases and barrels of whiskey line the docks in Nassau awaiting transfer to rumrunners who ferried the illegal booze into Florida and beyond. *Photo courtesy of "With the Whisky Smugglers," Flat Hammock Press.*

South Florida's coastline, with its abundance of secluded inlets, canals, coves, and mangrove swamps, coupled with the availability of adequate roadways providing easy pickup points and quick escapes, became the perfect setting for the importing and transporting of illegal alcohol. Flowing on the heels of the unlawful imports was cash—and plenty of it. Costing only four dollars at the original point of sale, a case of Cuban rum at the height of Prohibition sold for one hundred dollars or more once it hit Florida beaches.[20]

Anyone and everyone eager to make a quick buck ran his boat to and from the Bahamas hauling as much booze as his vessel could carry. Twenty-five-foot motorboats equipped with powerful engines were capable of carrying four hundred cases at a time. Thus, in the early years of Prohibition, acquiring and selling bootleg liquor from the Bahamas became a virtual free for all.[21]

To escape being caught in U.S. territorial waters, clever rum running entrepreneurs like William "Bill" McCoy, a boat builder from Holly Hills, Florida, purchased schooners, packed them full of liquor, and hovered along the East coast of the U.S. just outside the three mile territorial limit. Soon, other liquor-toting crafts joined him. This imaginary line with its bobbing heavy-laden vessels was dubbed "Rum Row." Smaller faster contact boats took the majority of the risk by ferrying booze from the larger vessels into the coast for private distribution or to speakeasies. Because of McCoy's dominance in the early part of the Prohibition era, he became the most notorious rum runner of all. Ironically, he was a teetotaler.[22]

Gertrude Lythgoe, distributor for a British distillery, crew hand, and William "Bill" McCoy, rumrunner, on the deck of McCoy's schooner *Arethusa* on Rum Row. *Photo courtesy of Flat Hammock Press.*

Torrio Brings in Capone

While booze was flowing freely into Florida from the Bahamas, back in Chicago, Torrio was just getting started with his rum running initiative. Wanting a savvy heavy weight that could assist in this new endeavor as well as run his myriad enterprises, Torrio promoted Capone to his chief assistant. His first job in this capacity was to move Outfit operations to Cicero, less than ten miles southwest of Chicago, where the gang's power of persuasion would be more pronounced. With fists full of cash and stimulus from Capone's brothers, Frank and Ralph, the Outfit's influence became prominent within police departments. Local government also fell when Capone had opposition election workers kidnapped and voters threatened by his henchmen who positioned themselves outside polling places sporting tommy guns. Some voters were actually shot and killed. In response, Chicago sent in police who gunned down Capone's brother Frank in the street.[23]

As part of his emerging image, Capone learned to present a congenial façade and keep his potentially explosive temper in check. Following the assault of his financial and legal advisor Jack "Greasy Thumb" Guzik (a.k.a. Jake Guzik) by freelance hijacker Joe Howard, however, Capone's twenty-five-year-old temper bubbled to the surface. He tracked down Guzik's assailant in Heinie Jacob's saloon and emptied his revolver into him. Lack of witnesses allowed Capone to get away with the murder.[24]

On January 24, 1925, Torrio was almost killed in Chicago by a spray of bullets and brutal assault from O'Banion's North Side gang. After recuperating in prison from his close call where he concurrently served time for Prohibition violations, Torrio had enough and decided to hang up his top gangster hat.[25] He closed a deal with Capone for a percentage of all illegal profits from his vast empire and told him, "It's all yours, Al." Torrio retired and left for Italy leaving Capone to succeed him as the Chicago Outfit's kingpin,[26] but not before the two took a little trip with their wives to Cuba.

Visiting Cuba by way of St. Petersburg, Florida

St. Petersburg, Florida, across the bay from Tampa, with its unspoiled Gulf Coast beaches, became a spot in which both Torrio and Capone invested their time and money. Torrio already had roots there, his mother- and brother-in-law having chosen the city as their home. In addition, Robert Vanella, "The Fox's" old associate from the James Street gang and for whom he was best man at his wedding, was now established in the area as a real estate agent. As for Capone, he was a baseball lover and personal friend of Yankee slugger Babe Ruth, and occasionally visited St. Petersburg where he watched The Babe hit home runs during spring training.[27]

Whatever enticed Capone to Florida—a familiar face on a baseball diamond, Florida's land boom, or all that new found money as Chicago's top gangster that was burning a hole in his pocket—he came to the Sunshine State at an opportune time and purchased several parcels of land both individually and as one of four partners in a company called the Manro Corporation. Other partners in the group included Johnny Torrio, Jack Guzik, and Robert Vanella, who represented Capone in the purchase of several parcels.

Ship's manifest from November 14, 1925, showing Torrio and Capone returning to Key West from Cuba. Image courtesy of National Archives.

18

It is presumed that when Torrio traveled through St. Petersburg in the fall of 1925 after his release from prison that arrangements were made for the establishment of the corporation and purchase of Florida's west coast land. This timing coincides with a manifest indicating Torrio's landing in Key West from Havana aboard the SS Cuba with his wife, Ann, Al Capone, and Mae on November 14, 1925.[28]

Parcels that Capone owned (several official records show his name as either Alphonse or Alphonso and his last name as Caponne), both individually or through the Manro Corporation were sprinkled throughout St. Petersburg. His individual investments included a 28-acre tract in South St. Petersburg bordering the town of Gulfport, now the site of the Twin Brooks Golf Course, and another large tract in Gulfport that went from 22nd Avenue South to 28th Avenue South, and 38th to 41st Street. He allegedly also held interest in property owned by Torrio in downtown St. Petersburg near the Green Cabin speakeasy.[29]

Of course, it wasn't just sunshine, baseball, or land that attracted Capone to Florida. At the height of Prohibition, the availability of illegal liquor was a huge draw. With Cuban rum flowing into the Florida Keys, British and Jamaican distilleries bringing booze into Nassau by the ship loads, and savvy entrepreneurs in their fast boats able to evade the Coast Guard, it was the perfect opportunity for him to arrange shipments of booze to his myriad Chicago speakeasies and plan expansion of his vast illicit empire. And it was his trips to Havana and others to the Bahamas that allowed him to make the necessary deals.

McCoy Nabbed, Mob Takes Over

By 1926, rum runner Bill McCoy had been caught by the Coast Guard for Prohibition violations and released after nine months in prison. During his incarceration, small time rumrunners were replaced by New York syndicates. With their well-established connections, modes of transportation, and generous handouts of cash bribes, these Yankees became thoroughly entrenched in the business of importing and selling illegal booze.

McCoy recalled in his biography *The Real McCoy*:

Nassau's invasion was composed of city men, New York City men, for the most part. Big shots of the underworld

19

and their escorts of gunmen and racketeers left their haunts in Manhattan and Brooklyn and moved to the Bahamas. The Nassau gang was largely made up of gangsters who knew gang procedure. They were not toughened and made reckless by what the boom compelled them to endure. They were more than adequately tough already. Big Eddie, Big Harry, Squinty, and Lefty, and the rest of them, poured in with their retinues of gorillas and for some vivid months proceeded to take Nassau apart and remold it closer to their heart's desire.

Bay Street, the waterfront chief thoroughfare of the town, no longer was a sun-drenched idle avenue where traffic sponges and sisal progressed torpidly. It was filled with slit-eyed, hunch-shouldered strangers, with the bluster of Manhattan in their voices and a wary truculence of manner. The faces that passed your shoulder in ten minutes on Bay Street would have given a New York cop nightmares for a week. Their owners, for the first few weeks, made existence a continual horror for the black constabulary of Nassau.[30]

Back in Chicago

After Torrio and Capone returned to Chicago from their trip to Cuba, Torrio left for the sunbathed shores of Italy. Capone, now running the Outfit, desired a more fashionable lifestyle so he moved his headquarters to Chicago's luxurious Metropole Hotel where he booked a five-room suite along with four guest rooms.[31]

To become more visible, he aggressively courted the press and attended high profile entertainment venues like the opera, a vestige from the old country considered by any respectable Italian to be the pinnacle of entertainment. To further stand out against the dull Chicago winters and dowdy attire of other gangsters, Capone wore custom-made suits accessorized by flamboyant and costly jewelry. This prompted his friends to call him "Snorky," meaning elegant. Fine cigars, gourmet food and drink, and female companionship became incessant indulgences.

The Chicago mobster basked in the limelight telling the press, "I am just a businessman, giving the people what they want" and desired to be viewed as a "respectable businessman and pillar of the community."[32] He ran his business enterprise, however, in quite the opposite fashion. Gambling, prostitution, and bootlegging enterprises were expanded exponentially by gunning down rivals.

With his enterprise in full swing, Capone imported huge quantities of liquor and beer readily supplying his establishments with variety and making him enormously rich. Numerous police raids of his brothels and gambling dens were ordered, but embarrassed customers and frightened employees refused to talk. The seemingly Teflon-coated gangster eluded incarceration again due to lack of evidence.

Capone surrounded himself with bodyguards from the Outfit wherever he went.

Newspaper reports of gangland activity unnerved law abiding citizens but with businessmen, politicians, and police on the "take," it appeared to be business as usual. Just around the corner, however, was an incident that would turn the tide of public opinion decidedly against Capone and gangland activity in general.

The Killing of Billy McSwiggin

On April 27, 1926, William "Billy" Harold McSwiggin, a popular assistant state attorney known as the "Hanging Prosecutor," was mistakenly shot and killed by Capone's hoodlums when they were gunning for rivals outside a saloon in Cicero. With blame placed squarely upon Capone, he immediately disappeared.

A series of police raids followed that included Cicero's bars, gambling dens, brothels, and Capone's hangouts. Included in the raids was the Hawthorne Smoke Shop directly across the street from Capone's headquarters. Police confiscated a number of items from the shop including several old notebooks. These would later prove to contain the incriminating evidence that would send Capone to prison.[33]

After three months of hiding, Capone returned, surrendered, and spent one night in jail. A subsequent investigation failed to turn up any witnesses or evidence of Capone's involvement in the killing; he escaped prosecution once again.[34] Following the McSwiggin incident, public outcry against gangster violence rose to a fevered pitch.

With the long cold winters of Chicago, harassment by the law, infighting among the various gangs, frequent liquor hijackings, and several attempts on his life, it's no wonder Capone sought the warmth and respite of South Florida. Having passed through the area on his way to and from Cuba on gambling junkets and liquor purchases, he called Miami, "the garden of America, the sunny Italy of the new world, where life is good and abundant, where happiness is to be had even by the poorest."[35] He looked forward to coming to the paradise of southern Florida with its warm sunshine, land ripe for investment, and promise of becoming a haven from his gangland problems.

Little did he know, however, that the latter would turn out to be merely a fairytale.

CHAPTER 2

FLORIDA LURES CAPONE

*I'm leaving for St. Petersburg, Florida, tomorrow. Let the
worthy citizens of Chicago get their liquor the best they can.
I'm sick of the job—it's a thankless one and full of grief. I
don't know when I'll be back, if ever . . . I've got some
property in St. Petersburg I want to sell . . . I wish all my
friends and enemies a Merry Christmas and a Happy New
Year. That's all they'll get from me this year. I hope I don't
spoil anybody's Christmas by not sticking around . . .*[36]

Al Capone

efore Capone came to South Florida, the land boom of the early
1920s, in which investors made millions, was at its height. Tourists
and potential land buyers occupied every hotel room in the area,
and the paradise to which they had traveled was filled with sun, fun,
booze, and gambling. Bankers, both in Florida and other states, soon
realized that the inflated land prices were due to speculators flipping the
properties. Eventually, banks became reluctant to provide backing for
these investments. Without these transactions, the economy of southern
Florida slowed to a crawl and eventually came to a screeching halt

altogether in 1926. Banks failed, businessmen lost fortunes, and families their livelihood. To add insult to injury, a devastating hurricane came through South Florida in the fall of 1926 and further ravaged the economy. By the time Capone moved to town in 1927, folks were ecstatic to have the "Capone outfit spread money like water at a time when business in every channel was depressed."[37]

Stopping in Deerfield

Marlin Eller met Al Capone in Deerfield, Florida, when he was twelve years old. His father, Hoyt Eller, had recently purchased a gas station and garage on the east side of Dixie Highway about 100 yards south of the Hillsboro Canal (where the Deerfield Beach city tennis courts are today). While Hoyt was busy getting his farm going west of town, Marlin was to man the station and pump gasoline for customers.

David Eller, Marlin's son and Deerfield Beach native, relates the story of his father's unexpected encounter with Al Capone:

> *One day a big black car filled with several men pulled in to get gas. The first time they stopped in they were coming from the north; the car had Illinois license plates. Dad heard Chicago mentioned, and they had a lot of inner tubes with tire punctures from the trip which needed to be patched. My Dad patched them for them, and when they picked up the tubes later on their way back north, the "boss man" of the group paid for the gas and tire patching, and then handed my father a $10 tip! This was a huge tip for a 12-year-old boy at the time. My Dad thought he was the nicest man in the world! But later on, when Al Capone was arrested and his picture was in the newspaper, my Dad saw the picture and realized who it was that had tipped him so generously.[38]*

Heading to Miami

Capone's stop in Deerfield (later to be called Deerfield Beach) occurred just prior to his announced arrival in Miami by the *Miami Daily News*. In a lengthy article, the newspaper quoted Capone as saying, "Miami's climate is more healthful than Chicago's and warmer than California—that's why I'm here."

The new arrival had just concluded a brief visit and abrupt departure from Los Angeles, California. When asked why he left The Golden State so suddenly, he told reporters: "When I got in [to Los Angeles], a bunch of the boys [his gang] met me at the train. Some of them must have had guns on their hips and the police didn't like that, so they thought I was a bad moral influence or something. They had me all wrong there, and I'm glad to say my reception here has been quite different."

Quite different indeed! Upon arriving in Miami, Capone, escorted by a friend but minus his typical company of three Chicago bodyguards, walked to police headquarters from his hotel just before noon. There, he asked for Chief of Police Leslie Quigg and let him know he was merely in Miami as a "sun-hunter." His arrival at police headquarters attracted little or no attention, but in short order a crowd developed. The *Miami Daily News* described the scene:

Capone wore a blue suit and gray fedora hat. He did not wear any excess jewelry. He combs his wavy black hair straight back from his forehead. He is rather heavyset and does not look older than 30 . . . he stuffed his hands deep into the pockets of his neatly creased blue serge trousers and beamed affectionately at the welcoming committee of bluecoats and newspapermen.

Capone told reporters that he came to the station to "lay his cards face up on the table" and all he was down here for was rest and vacation. Quigg informed reporters that Capone should be treated as any other winter visitor.

Along with relaxation, Capone said that he also planned to make some real estate investments, but he assured the chief that he would refrain from engaging in "business."[39] That promise didn't last long. The next day's *Miami Daily News* suggested quite a different story. Under the headline "Capone Denies Tim Murphy is Prospective Aid," the paper stated that Chicago dispatches had reported that Capone and Timothy D. "Big Tim" Murphy, another Chicago mobster and labor racketeer who controlled several major railroad, laundry, and dye worker's unions,[40] were in discussions in Miami. The topic of the supposed conference was whether Big Tim would act as "prime minister" and "fixer" of the Outfit during the mob boss's absence from Chicago. Capone, whom reporters said was difficult to reach at his downtown hotel where he had taken up almost half the floor, denied allegations and told the press he had, "absolutely nothing to do with Murphy."[41]

While he may have been truthful about not engaging Murphy as his temporary replacement in Chicago, his rhetoric regarding his promise not to establish any businesses in the area was like a sieve; it didn't hold water. Just forty-five miles north of the city in the small town of Deerfield, something fishy was taking place.

Capone's Little "Fish" Business

According to David Eller, third generation Deerfield Beach resident, Capone had a little "fish" business where the Florida East Coast Canal, now the Intracoastal Waterway, intersects the Hillsboro Canal. Local fishermen were contracted to bring in their catch, then under the cloak of darkness, they would stash illegal booze brought in from the Bahamas into large watertight containers, place a false bottom over the bottles, and pack the rest of the container with dry ice and fish. The containers were subsequently delivered to the Florida East Coast (FEC) railroad station, not far from the business, for shipment to Chicago.

During Prohibition, what eventually became the Riverview restaurant served as Al Capone's Deerfield speakeasy. *Photo courtesy of the Deerfield Beach Historical Society.*

Along with his fish business, Capone owned a gambling house and speakeasy in the same vicinity. Eller's grandmother, Mattie Eller, an "excellent seamstress," told the family that she used to earn extra money "making dresses for the girls who worked at Mr. Capone's private establishment."

Eller stated that after Capone's later conviction on tax evasion and subsequent incarceration, his speakeasy was put up for auction. "It was bought by Mr. Bill Stewart [who managed the speakeasy for Capone] who reopened it as a public restaurant which he named Riverview. He operated it from the 30s to the 50s when he died and left it to his nephew, also named Bill Stewart, who was a good friend of mine.[42]

Walls in the Riverview restaurant were decorated with the old leftover gambling paraphernalia and was considered the premier restaurant in town from the 60s to the 80s. It specialized in Florida lobster, local fish, and, according to Eller, "the best steaks in South Florida!"

Unfortunately, the building was damaged beyond repair in dual hurricanes Frances and Jeanne in 2004 and was demolished in 2005. Today, the land on which the Riverview sat, as well as adjacent land, is slated to become an expanded Sullivan Park for Deerfield Beach residents. Renderings of the facility include walkways, fountains, boat docks, a children's playground, and picnic area.[43] Deerfield Island, once known as Capone Island and located directly across the canal, is accessible only from this park. (More about Capone Island later.)

The success of Capone's speakeasy in Deerfield and that of his other Chicago enterprises depended upon the accessibility of booze, and plenty of it. To satisfy the need of his thirsty customers, Capone made deals with distributors in the Bahamas and built a highly reliable transportation network.

Toting the Booze

In the early years of Prohibition, illegal booze was brought into Florida by boat from the Bahamas. By the mid-1920s, however, an expanded Coast Guard presence with its faster vessels and stepped up methods of communication, including coded radio transmissions, forced rum runners to develop a quicker and more economical way to import their illegal booty. This ushered in the need for land and sea planes, pilots, and the establishment of obscure airstrips in remote locations along Florida's east coast and beyond.

One of the "legitimate" airlines operating out of South Florida at the time was Chalk Ocean Airways. Arthur B. "Pappy" Chalk, owner of the airline, had been an auto mechanic from Paducah, Kentucky, before moving to Miami and starting his ad hoc charter service of sea planes. As early as 1919, Chalks was ferrying passengers and cargo to and from the Bahamas on a regular basis. During Prohibition, it was not uncommon for passengers to include both booze smugglers, including Capone, and the revenue agents that chased them. Many times, legitimate cargo was mixed with the illegal potable variety. Soon, transporting forbidden alcohol by air became more efficient and economical for the buyer, and quite lucrative for the pilots. It wasn't long before private pilots with their land and sea planes were in high demand.[44]

Flying Ace for Capone

Robert Hanley was an adolescent growing up in Miami when the flying bug bit him. His parents had taken him to the fairgrounds near Coral Gables where, for the first time, he watched barnstormers dazzle spectators in a daring air show. His stomach churned with excitement as he stood mesmerized by the aircrafts and the stunts their thrill-seeking pilots performed—loop-the-loops, barrel rolls, dives, and spins. Right then and there he knew beyond any shadow of a doubt that he wanted to fly. Not even his viewing an explosive crash in which the pilot burned to death in the cockpit of his plane would squelch young Hanley's new found enthusiasm.

By his mid-teens, Hanley had learned to fly by hanging out with airplane mechanics and pilots at a small Miami airport after school. It was here he took his first solo flight in a Swallow biplane. At the age of seventeen, he was juggling high school at St. Patrick, a private Catholic school on Miami Beach, his time at the airport, and his part-time job working as a busboy in a Miami restaurant. It was there that he met the infamous Al Capone.

Hearing that young Hanley was a pilot, Capone asked him whether he'd be interested in transporting certain "cargo" from the Bahamas back to Miami. What could be more exciting than to actually get paid big bucks to do what he loved? Hanley took the job.

The teen had butterflies in his stomach when he lied to his parents on a Friday afternoon that he was going to visit his friend Freddy in Hollywood (about 20 miles north) for the weekend. Instead, dressed like an adventuresome flyer—complete with fancy shirt, scarf, jacket, and leather boots—he went downtown and caught the *Bahamas Boat*, a ferry service from the Florida mainland to the Bahamas. The five hour journey landed him at West End on the isle of Grand Bahama.

As a teen, Robert Hanley flew liquor into Florida for Al Capone. *Photo courtesy of Stuart Hanley.*

On Saturday, he spent most of the day checking out the plane he would fly, a single-engine Commandaire biplane on floats. At dusk, wearing goggles and a helmet and flying a plane full of forbidden booze, Hanley, and several other pilots, headed to Florida. It was the young pilot's first experience flying at night. An hour and ten minutes later, the planes arrived in Biscayne Bay at around 125th Street where Hanley delivered his first load—twenty-six cases of whiskey.

"We'd land at Bay Point in the water and taxi on up to a little sort of a beach, very, very sandy, and stop," he wrote in his memoires.[45] The booze was then transported by uniformed servants to an upscale home in the neighborhood.

On subsequent weekends, with his parents none the wiser, Hanley flew as many as five loads a night and was paid as much as $300 a load, depending on the plane he flew and the amount of cargo it carried. After delivering the "goods," he hung out at The Cockpit, a speakeasy in northwest Miami where he mingled with other aviators and rum runners. Upon returning home, he'd stuff the proceeds from his trips under his mattress.

Occasionally he flew Sunday nights as well, returning to Miami on Monday morning, always late for school. On one such Sunday run, Hanley, with less than 200 flying hours, had taxied up onto the beach. The plane was being off loaded when all of a sudden one of the workers shouted, "Hey! Get goin! Get outta here!" Then the cargo hatch slammed shut. Someone had blown the whistle on the couriers.

Hanley immediately taxied into the bay. Unfortunately, he was headed right into the path of an oncoming Coast Guard cutter. While he made it into the air, his enlarged young ego got the better of him. Instead of turning out to sea, he did a 180, thumbed his nose at the cutter, and buzzed it. The next thing he heard was a loud BOOM! Then his leg felt as though it had been struck by a sledgehammer.

The young aviator instinctively knew that he'd been hit by one of the bullets from the barrage of gunfire that had emanated from the Coast Guard cutter, but he didn't know exactly where the bullet had lodged. He could feel a warm liquid running down his leg and put his hand into his boot. It came up wet. He grabbed his flashlight and flicked it on. To his horror, the side of his pants was saturated with blood. Hanley's only thought was to head east to West End.

"I remember praying and feeling groggy like I was going to faint and got down close to the water. That's all I remember," wrote Hanley.

The young flier's parents were frantic when he didn't show up for school on Monday. Hanley's girlfriend Catherine, whose father was head of Customs, told them that he'd been shot down by the Coast Guard and that it would be best to speak with the Syndicate (Capone). Hanley's mother did just that.

Capone left no stone unturned in an effort to find his downed pilot. His men contacted their sources, and shortly thereafter Hanley's parents were told. "Well, the latest word we have is he's all right and he's on a boat and he's got a bullet hole in his leg."

Capone's men had found Hanley in a mangrove swamp miles from West End, the plane's propeller still engaged. They transported the unconscious pilot by speedboat to Capone's base just off Bimini, an old wreck of a ship called the SS Sapona.[46]

The concrete vessel was a Liberty ship that had been built as a cargo steamer at the end of World War I. After it was decommissioned, it was purchased by Carl G. Fisher in the early 1920s who traded her engine and machinery to a dredging company in exchange for dredging work during his development of Miami Beach.

In April 1924, Bruce Bethel, a British officer who had retired to Bimini after losing an arm in World War I, purchased the vessel from Fisher and towed it to Bimini where he turned it into a floating warehouse for the storage of rum and whiskey.[47] It also housed Capone's combination distillery, warehouse, and hospital. It was here that Hanley's bullet was removed and his leg patched up. Afterwards, he was taken back to West End.

Robert Hanley was taken to the SS Sapona to receive medical treatment for his gunshot wound. The stern of the ship broke off during the 1926 hurricane. *Photo courtesy of Broward County Historical Commission.*

Hanley's father contacted the Coast Guard who ferried the wrought parent over to the islands to pick up his son. Back in school and on crutches, word that Bob Hanley was a rumrunner and had been shot resulted in a bolstered reputation which he enjoyed for many years. (He kept the extracted bullet, a 30-06, as a souvenir until it was lost years later in a fire in Jamaica.)

This harrowing incident should have ended young Hanley's rum running career. It didn't. He continued to fly when the demand for booze was high. On one such run in a land plane, he was supposed to off-load his cargo of 115 cases of whiskey at an obscure inland airfield. As he flew over the landing zone, however, he spied government agents waiting for him. Aborting his mission, he headed his Fairchild 71C north along the coast. A Coast Guard aircraft followed in hot pursuit and chased him all the way to Georgia.

Daylight turned to dusk and Hanley's plane was running out of fuel. He desperately needed to land. Selecting the first field he found that looked smooth, he set down. Unfortunately, it was in a newly ploughed cornfield. The rough landing coupled with the heavy cargo collapsed the landing gear, and the aircraft skidded on her belly across the furrows to a stop.

Working into the wee hours of the morning, the resident farmer helped Hanley unload the liquor and remove the plane's engine and instruments. Siphoning what was left of the plane's fuel, Hanley doused the wooden craft and set it ablaze, a sad event for him since it was a fairly new aircraft with less than one hundred hours on her. He then phoned Capone to let him know that he and the cargo were still intact.

The next night, a truck and big black car arrived at the farm. The first ferried the rescued booze to Capone's enterprises; the second carried Hanley back to Miami. Frank "The Enforcer" Nitti, Capone's second in command, met Hanley in Miami and told him, "You did such a beautiful job we'd like you to take it easy for a while and lay low." He handed the teen $2,000 in cash (almost $30,000 today!).

After upwards of eighty runs, Hanley retired from the business of rum running. Proceeds from his short-lived but lucrative career paid for a car, his college education, and then some. It also gave him the experience and impetus he needed to make flying his career.[48]

CHAPTER 3

CAPONE BECOMES ENTRENCHED IN MIAMI

The country wanted booze, and I organized it. Why should I be called a "public enemy?"[49]

Al Capone

Capone often stayed in local high end hotels while passing through Miami on his way to and from Cuba and the Bahamas to vacation or contract for the importation of liquor. The earliest record of any semblance of roots in the Miami area, however, comes from a report by Internal Revenue agent Frank Wilson. He wrote that in 1927 Al and his wife Mae rented a house from the Sterns at 3605 Indian Creek Drive on Miami Beach. The price for the six month season (typically November to April) was $2,500. Capone coughed up the down payment of between $800 and $900 in one hundred dollar bills.[50]

Since Capone had rented the home under the name "Al Brown," an alias he used on numerous occasions, the Sterns had no idea they had actually rented their dwelling to the infamous gangster. In fact, it wasn't until they were on their way to the Riviera and heard a news flash on a ship's radio that they realized what had transpired. Believing they would find their home in shambles upon their return, the Sterns were astounded to find not even one tiny scratch on their furniture or accessories. They were equally surprised to discover that the Capones had doubled the size of most of their silver and china upon finding its quantity insufficient for the number of guests they entertained. Yet an unpaid $400 phone bill remained. Mae later returned and gave the Sterns a $500 bill. Realizing that the couple was unable to make change, Mae simply told them to keep it.

Capone maintained his headquarters in the penthouse suite atop the Ponce de Leon Hotel. *(ca. 1924) Photo courtesy of State Archives of Florida, Florida Memory. Gleason Waite Romer photographer.*

During the time that the Capone's rented from the Sterns, Al also maintained headquarters in penthouse suite #804 atop the Ponce de Leon hotel at 231 East Flagler Street in Miami. Not wanting to use his real name, he registered under the name "A. Costa."[51]

Parker Adair Henderson, Jr., son of former Miami mayor Parker Adair "P.A." Henderson, ran the hotel and did everything possible to please his new guest. After all, how could he not? With Capone in the hotel, the dining room transitioned from a losing proposition into a complete financial success.

"Each night Capone would tender a banquet for friends. He would order food for about 50 people, and probably there would be only about seven or eight at the table. When we would present the check, Capone would refuse to pay it unless we doubled it. When we would abide by his wishes, he would pull out a large bill and the waiters would keep the change," recalled Henderson.[52]

Capitalizing on the manager's obvious infatuation with the gangster and his lifestyle, Capone invited Henderson to his suite, introduced him to his gun totting entourage, and even had him as a guest at this Indian Creek rental, all while cultivating him for more "important" tasks.

So eager was Henderson to align himself with the gangster that from January 14 until April 2, 1928, he, along with Nick Circella, one of Capone's armed bodyguards, picked up money orders from Western Union totaling $31,000. The checks, made out to "Albert Costa," were endorsed by Henderson under the fictitious name.[53]

But that wouldn't be all that Henderson would do for Capone. Two important purchases were about to be made by Capone's willing agent.

Henderson's First Purchase

Henderson thought he was doing Capone a favor when he was asked to purchase twelve guns for the mob boss and bring them to his room. After accepting cash to procure the weapons, Henderson walked into a North Miami Avenue pawn shop, bought the firearms, and returned to Capone's hotel room only to find it deserted. Dutifully, he laid the weapons on the bed and walked out. Returning to the room several hours later, he found it equally deserted including the guns. Concerned that

Capone would not look kindly upon the disappearance of the firearms, the next time Henderson saw Capone he told him what had happened. "That's all right, Parker, the deal was o.k.," Henderson quoted Capone as saying.[54]

One of the handguns, an automatic pistol, was later found in New York City in an abandoned car with Tennessee license plates after the assassination of Frankie Yale, Capone's former mentor turned rival. Yale, who had been shot down behind the wheel of his car near his home in Brooklyn, New York, had fallen out of favor with Capone when he double crossed the Outfit boss in a liquor deal.

Prior to the murder, Jack Guzik, now Capone's chief lieutenant, Charles Fachetti, a notorious Chicago gunman, and Sherri Tellin, a member of Capone's gang, had been regulars at Capone's Miami headquarters. On June 29, 1928, Capone had accompanied the three men to the Florida East Coast railroad station where the gang members bought tickets to Chicago. They left on July 1 aboard the Havana Special, a New York train that was due into Manhattan Sunday morning. Several hours later, Frankie Yale was dead, his body riddled with bullets from the weapons of four gunmen in a passing car. Capone, still in Miami, was subsequently questioned by authorities about the murder. He, of course, knew nothing.

One of the guns used in the slaying was eventually traced to Henderson through the serial number. He gave authorities a sworn statement in which he confessed to buying the weapons, but said he had no idea for what they would be used. Later, he was accompanied to New York by Miami Police Chief Guy Reeve "strictly for protection" where he further supplemented this statement regarding purchase of the weapons in discussions with District Attorney Dodd and New York police. Satisfied that Henderson was in Asheville, North Carolina, during Yale's slaying, police did not arrest him.[55]

Outfit Moves to Hotel Lexington

Capone frequently returned to Chicago to conduct the Outfit's business. In late July 1928, after numerous police raids at the Metropole hotel following Yale's murder, Capone moved his headquarters one block north to the Hotel Lexington. The hotel had deteriorated substantially since President S. Grover Cleveland stayed in it when he came to open the Columbian Exposition, a World's Fair held in Chicago in 1893 to celebrate the 400th anniversary of Christopher Columbus's arrival in the New

World. Yet despite the questionable setting, Capone and his associates occupied as many as 54 rooms, taking up the entire fourth floor and most of the third.[56] In his "office," Capone sat, back to the window, in a steel-backed chair.[57]

It was no secret that Capone availed himself of female companionship throughout his career, changing women when the mood struck. With his move to the Lexington, he added a number of rooms throughout the hotel for the gang's women, and included one room on the fifth floor for his latest companion, a teenage blond Greek. Concerned about a vaginal lesion, the teen sought medical counsel from David V. Omens, Capone's doctor. A Wasserman test that was administered came back positive—she had syphilis. Whether Capone was ever treated at this time is unknown.[58] What is known, however, is that the consequences of his multiple dalliances later came back to haunt him.

Revenge Killings

The Yale murder set off a series of revenge killings. Members of Yale's former gang, along with Chicago bootlegger and organized crime leader Joe Aiello, who maintained an ongoing and bloody feud with Capone, gunned down two of Capone's associates. Tony Lombardo, Capone's handpicked president of the Unione Siciliana, a fraternal organization that controlled much of the Italian-American vote, was the first victim. He was ambushed on September 7, 1928. His successor, Pasqualino Lolordo, also a friend of Capone's, was gunned down on January 8, 1929. Two of Lolordo's killers were Pete and Frank Gusenberg, the best gunmen in the dwindling North Side gang headed by George "Bugs" Moran. After the killings, Capone, who was in a constant turf war with Moran, returned to Miami, but he now had the rival in his crosshairs.[59]

As Capone planned a reprisal from his Miami hotel suite, Henderson was eager to suggest more permanent living arrangements for his most important hotel guest.

Henderson's Second Purchase

Henderson, along with Miami Beach Mayor John Newton Lummus, Jr., who was a realtor, clandestinely approached Capone about looking for a residence on Miami Beach. While not really interested in owning another home, Capone consented to look at a few. One of the homes Henderson and Lummus showed him was on Palm Island.

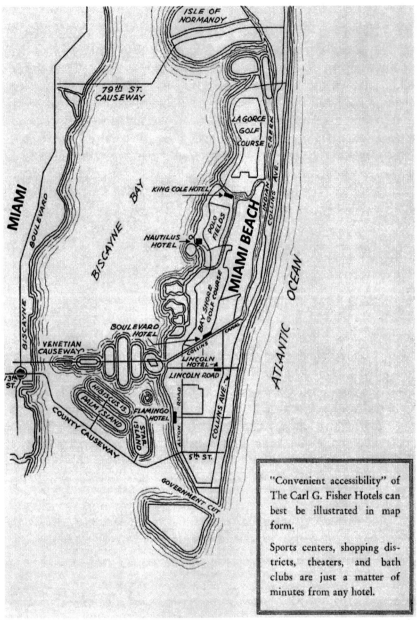

"Convenient accessibility" of The Carl G. Fisher Hotels can best be illustrated in map form.

Sports centers, shopping districts, theaters, and bath clubs are just a matter of minutes from any hotel.

This map from the 1930s locates the five Carl Fisher hotels. It also gives a good overview of the locations of Miami, Miami Beach, Palm, Hibiscus and Star Islands, as well as the 79th Street and County Causeways. *Image courtesy of Miami Beach Historic Archives.*

The city of Miami Beach sits across Biscayne Bay from Miami and consists of a series of islands. Among these are Miami Beach, the largest island, and a number of smaller islands that include Palm, Hibiscus, and Star Islands. In 1919, the Biscayne Bay Islands Company with Lock T. Highleyman listed as president, purchased submerged land on the north side of what was then known as County Causeway (now MacArthur Causeway) and pumped sand from the bay to create two parallel islands. Palm Island was completed in 1921; neighboring Hibiscus Island was completed in 1924.[60]

Clarence Marshall Busch (1860-1943), *not* associated with the Anheuser Busch family, was from Philadelphia. His occupation in the 1880 U.S. Census listed him as a "bookbinder."[61] He eventually became state printer for the state of Pennsylvania gaining him great wealth in the process.[62] It is unknown just when he retired from the printing business and turned his attention to real estate, but he sold many large mansions on Long Island and Atlantic City thereby increasing his prosperity. By 1910 at age 40, he was living with his wife, Bonnie, and young daughter, Violet, in Great Neck, New York.[63] In the winter, he traveled to Miami with Bonnie, a novelist and President of the Society of American Pen Women.[64] A staunch Prohibitionist, Bonnie had voiced her opinion prior to enactment of the 18th Amendment stating she was glad to "underwrite prohibition, the moral life insurance of our nation" and pleaded for "sober judges, clear headed statesmen and unswerving public to keep our nation from failing."[65]

Busch built his first Florida home on Miami's Brickell Avenue. He sold that house and all its "costly antiques from the four corners of the globe" to showgirl and renowned gold digger Peggy Hopkins Joyce in 1920 for close to $200,000.[66] The next year, Busch and Lock T. Highleyman developed Palm Island. The two men had known each other for years having served as officers of the Fidelity Bank and Trust Company in Miami (Highleyman as President, Busch as First Vice President).[67] The bank had formed in 1916 and closed its doors in 1921.[68]

As celebrated developer of the Palm Island community, Busch built his own home at 94 Palm Avenue on the west shore of the island for $75,000. Highleyman lived two houses down.[69] One of the next houses Busch built as an investment was located at 93 Palm Avenue, directly across the street from his own home. Completed in 1922, the Spanish Style two-story home had a living area of 6,103 square feet that included seven bedrooms, five full baths, and two half baths. It sat on the east side of the island and ran 300 feet back to the bay. The back yard had water frontage of 100 feet and a commanding view of Hibiscus Island across the bay.[70] Its first owner was insurance broker James W. Popham.

Clarence Busch (above) and Lock T. Highleyman developed Palm and Hibiscus Islands in 1921. Busch built his home at 94 Palm Avenue for $75,000. He built another investment home at 93 Palm Avenue, directly across the street. Al Capone eventually purchased that home in 1928. *Photo courtesy of Dawn McMillan.*

When Popham decided to build a new home on Star Island, he engaged Busch as his real estate agent to sell his Palm Island home. With Parker Henderson, Jr., acting as agent for the undisclosed buyer, little did Busch know he had actually sold the home to the notorious gangster Al Capone.[71]

Al Capone had a 30- by 60-foot pool built at his home at 93 Palm Avenue. At the time, it was the largest private pool in Florida. *Photo courtesy of State Archives of Florida.*

Although thrilled to have sold his home, Popham was livid when he discovered that Capone was the new owner of the house. In fact, Popham later brought a foreclosure suit against both Parker A. Henderson and Mae Capone, joined by her husband Al. The suit stated that Henderson had agreed to purchase the property from Popham for $30,000 and that he had signed three promissory notes for $10,000 each but that the defendants had "failed and refused to pay this indebtedness or any part of it."[72] Six months after closing on the property, Henderson signed the deed over to Mae Capone.[73]

Henderson Continues to Agent for Capone

Henderson's role as Capone's gofer didn't stop at the purchase of guns or that of 93 Palm Avenue. Records in the office of the Miami Beach building inspector showed that while Capone was in Chicago for the local primary and to make plans for his permanent move to Miami, permits for the construction of a swimming pool and a wall to surround the compound were taken out by Henderson. The 30- by 60-foot swimming pool proved to be the largest privately owned pool in Florida at the time.[74]

Improvements to the home also included mosaic walkways, rock gardens, and fountains constructed by the finest artisans available. Capone expected the best and in order to get it, he went beyond the call. One day a crew of tile layers breaking for lunch found their lunch pails had vanished. Instead of their usual homemade sandwiches and fruit, they were invited into the Capone house for a gigantic feast. The welcomed lunchtime spread was repeated each day.[75]

Word of Capone's financial generosity quickly spread around town. Soon, merchants and respectable businessmen vied for his attention and lavish spending.

CHAPTER 4

MONEY CAN'T BUY HAPPINESS

*I'm a business man. I've made my money supplying a popular
demand. If I break the law, my customers
are as guilty as I am.*[76]

Al Capone

Local restauranteurs loved the money Capone extravagantly spent when in their establishments, and servers, car hops, and hospitality workers swooned over his $100 tips. Even retailers wooed the generous spender. One such retailer was Sewell Brothers' Store, a haberdashery.

Capone, accompanied by local gambler Skeets Downs, was introduced to Sewells by Parker Henderson. After purchasing $1,000 worth of "suits, shirts, underwear, ties by the handful, shoes and socks, the kind of clothes that would make him look like a tourist," Jack Sewell gave Capone a free belt and hat as a bonus. Capone was so impressed—"It's the first time anyone ever gave me anything free."—that whenever anyone in his gang shopped for clothes, they went to Sewells.[77]

While retailer's profited from Capone's presence, residents weren't ready for the infamous hoodlum to settle in their back yard. When word got out of the sale of 93 Palm Avenue to the notorious Chicago mobster, outrage spread like wildfire.

Unwelcomed Resident

Capone was in Chicago when, on June 27, 1928, a meeting was called between city officials and law enforcement officers of Miami, Miami Beach, and Dade County along with Palm Island residents to discuss at length the gangster's presence in the Miami area and his recent purchase of the Palm Island estate. In what was described as a "stormy session," the rhetoric was quite heated. Verbal insults and accusations of wrongdoing and fraud were hurled at Miami's mayor Lummus for "bringing Capone back to the city" and "condoning the presence of the mobster." They also noted that with Parker Henderson acting as "straw man," Lummus had even collected a real estate commission from the sale of the Palm Island home. Livid at the mayor's actions, several men bellowed for his removal.

During the impassioned discussion, John Orr, who owned a home just down the street from Capone, was one of the outspoken Palm Island residents. He, along with others in the Palm and Hibiscus Islands Improvement Association, presented a resolution calling for endorsement by the City Council to ". . . take such steps as may be within its power and cooperate in every way possible with all law enforcement officers of Dade County and the various municipalities of this area to the end that this said Al Capone be no longer a resident of this community." In the end, Lummus, who admitted no wrongdoing, denounced the resolution stating that they had no right to arrest Capone without just cause. The declaration, however, passed unanimously with the backing of Miami Beach citizens as a whole.

County Solicitor Robert Taylor directed Henderson to tell Capone not to return to Miami. Henderson subsequently traveled to Chicago to deliver the message but returned saying that Capone would not listen and that he insisted that he was in Miami for his health and had no criminal intentions. He also fervently explained that he had invested a sizeable amount of money in his residence and that, "he was a citizen and taxpayer and would take his case to stay in Miami all the way to the U.S. Supreme Court if necessary."[78]

Neighbors Voice their Outrage

Capone was enthralled with his new home and subsequent improvements, but others were infuriated. A letter sent to Florida's Governor Doyle E. Carlton by Palm Island developer and resident Clarence Busch spoke of the extensive and unauthorized $70,000 worth of renovations made to the Capone property. (See appendix for additional information on the design and architecture of the home.) It further explained the negative impact the Capone purchase had on residents and property values.

> He has built on piling a solid concrete wall surrounding the property and which is about seven feet high. The two front entrances are enclosed by high iron gates. The small one car, one story garage fronting on the Avenue on the West side of the lot, has been replaced by a large two story lodge house covering the driveway also, the second floor rooms of which command the road. At the water front he has erected a dock larger than any in this vicinity and big enough for a small sized ferry boat. On the land adjoining the dock he has built a high two story structure, ostensibly a diving pavillon [sic], but the second floor enclosed rooms of it command the water in all directions . . . I think it can be said that every one of the nine other residences on the East half of Palm Island is for sale and almost every one was built by the occupant for a permanent home. The restrictions which run with the land prohibit any boat house or structure on the water front of a greater height than eight feet. This building of his must be nearly or quite 25 feet high, but the Island Company is too terrorized to object . . .

Busch went on to write that a sizeable "For Sale" sign was being displayed in the lot adjoining Capone's and that the mindset of most of the residents on the east half of the island was "fright and flight." He continued: "It is not a question of depreciation of the property, he has simply killed the sale of any price of residences with a cost value of over a million and reduced by 50% or more the value of the 24 remaining lots, say $240,000."

Besides the drop in property values and dead sales, a three-month renter across from Capone's compound who paid a considerable amount of money for his accommodations complained of an exorbitant amount of "racket" emanating from the Capone residence. This included all night parties and the shooting of firearms. The complaint prompted Busch to write a letter to Capone. In it he stated that while these disturbances may be happening "possibly in your absence," curtailing these activities would allow residents to have "quiet about their homes, especially at night." Busch included a copy of his correspondence to Capone in his letter to the governor which ended with a plea for the governor to keep the correspondence with Capone private so it would not reach the "enemy."

While Busch's letter to Capone did the trick and there were no further complaints, the tenant vacated the premises after just two months.[79] The renter's unexpected encounter with Capone would be repeated by many others in the area.

When called to the home of an ill Miami Beach citizen, Dr. Homer Lee Pearson Jr. was flabbergasted to find out his patient was Al Capone. *Photo courtesy of Reverend Lee Pearson, III.*

A Surprise Encounter

Dr. Homer Lee Pearson Jr., who, along with his wife had moved from Georgia to Miami in 1924, practiced in an office in the DuPont Building in the late 1920s. While at home one night, Dr. Pearson received a phone call from a man with a deep raspy voice.

Reverend Lee Pearson, a Miami native and son of the physician, recalled what happened next: "The man said he had a friend who needed to see a doctor. Still in the days of house calls, my father agreed to go see him and asked for the address. The man said he would have someone pick my dad up and take him to the patient. A while later, a big black car pulled up. When they arrived at the patient's home, Dad was ushered in and there was Al Capone lying on a couch. He might have had a cold or the flu. What was said or what was done or prescribed I have no idea. After a few minutes Dad said they paid him in cash and took him back home. As far as I know, it never came up again, except for probable bragging at school by me."

Ironically, Dr. Pearson wasn't a family doctor or Internist; he was an OB/GYN.[80]

Capone's Neighbors: Clarence Busch and John B. Orr Sr.

Dawn McMillan, granddaughter of Clarence and Bonnie Busch, recalled stories her mother Barbara told her about the family's experiences while living across the street from the infamous Al Capone on Palm Island.

In one such story, Barbara had a pet raccoon named Boots. Being nocturnal, Boots liked to roam at night with his favorite wanderings taking him over the high wall surrounding the Capone home. While investigating the grounds, he would make it over to the dog's bowl and chow down on whatever food had been left out for the canine. On this particular night, one of Capone's henchmen came over to the Busch house and told Barbara in no uncertain terms that, "If we see that raccoon over there one more time we're going to kill him." Not wanting that to happen to her beloved pet, Barbara took Boots out to the Everglades and released him.

Another time, the Busch family thought they heard a prowler outside their home and called on Capone for assistance. "Al's henchmen came over with their tommy guns and searched the yard. Luckily, they didn't find anyone," Barbara told her daughter.

A final story Dawn recalls is one remembered by an elderly female cousin who visited Palm Island. She recalled that Dawn's brother Leslie, twenty years her senior, would sit on the balcony of the Palm Island home and shoot pebbles at Al Capone's guards with a sling shot. "Brave boy!" she concluded.[81]

Barbara Busch and pet raccoon Boots. *Photo courtesy of Dawn McMillan.*

John B. Orr Sr., a prominent builder and pillar of the Miami community, lived on Palm Island (49 Palm Avenue), just down the street from Capone. He worked on such structures as John Deering's Vizcaya and his buildings include the Miami Biltmore Hotel, Everglades Club in Palm Beach, his own home on Palm Island, as well as numerous other high end homes and commercial structures in Florida.[82] His son, John B. Orr Jr., who later became an attorney, served in the Florida Legislature and went on to become Mayor of Dade County, grew up on Palm Island. When John Orr Jr. had children of his own, he told his son Tom of a harrowing encounter he had one night at 93 Palm Avenue, one that could have had a tragic outcome.

While in high school, John B. Orr Jr. and his girlfriend were out on a date in his ski boat anchored just off their backyard on Palm Island. With their eyes and romantic attentions on each other, little did they realize that the boat anchor had lifted. John Orr Jr. told Tom: "All of a sudden, lights came on everywhere and lit up the water. Then we saw men in suits running onto a dock pointing tommy guns at us. After a minute, a man came out and said, 'Aw, it's just the kids from next door.' Unbeknownst to us, we had drifted up to Capone's house!"[83]

Having unexpectedly encountered Capone's bodyguards, perhaps the teens should have attended the town hall meeting given by Miami's Police Chief Guy C. Reeve.

John B. Orr Sr., builder and resident of Palm Island (above), was a staunch opponent of Capone's presence in Miami Beach. John B. Orr Jr. (inset) had an encounter with Capone's bodyguards. *Photo courtesy of Carol Orr Hartman.*

Minding your Ps and Qs around Capone's Bodyguards

Miami as well as Miami Beach residents had never seen anyone like Capone, someone who strode down streets, ate at restaurants, and availed himself of Miami attractions, illegal or otherwise, encased in bodyguards. So disturbed was the public about the possibility of encountering one of Capone's thugs on the street and unknowingly angering him, they asked Police Chief Reeve, who had served in the department of justice before coming to Miami, to give them a brief lesson on bodyguard etiquette.

In a town hall meeting, the police chief answered myriad questions from his audience such as: What is a bodyguard? Why does someone need a bodyguard? Are they usually armed? How would a bodyguard act in case of trouble? The Chief responded to each question with a brief pointed answer that helped residents prepare in case of a chance meeting.[84]

St. Valentine's Day Massacre

Far from the balmy nights of Miami Beach and Capone's enjoyment of same, Chicago's gangs continued to engage in narcotics trafficking, gambling, and prostitution. By 1929, however, Capone and other big-time gangsters had become thoroughly entrenched in the illegal liquor business. Hijackings and double crossings were commonplace, and disagreements typically resulted in death by rival gunmen who looked upon such murders as simply "part of the business."

On February 14, 1929, an overcast sky blotted out the morning sun and a brisk wind tossed snowflakes through the Windy City of Chicago. Inside the SMC Cartage Company, a brick warehouse at 2122 North Clark Street, several of George "Bugs" Moran's gang—Frank and Pete Gusenberg (who had murdered Capone's political allies), James Clark, Adam Heyer, and Al Weinshank—talked quietly while waiting for a truckload of hijacked whiskey. A sixth man, an optometrist, had tagged along to rub shoulders with the gang and watch the operation. Over to the side, Johnny May, an ex-safecracker and auto mechanic, was tinkering with his truck; his Alsatian dog Highball was tied to the bumper.[85]

As the men waited, a Cadillac, which resembled a Chicago detective squad car complete with "a siren, running-board gong and gun rack behind the driver's seat," pulled to the curb outside the warehouse. Two men in police uniforms and two others in civilian clothes left the vehicle and entered the warehouse, leaving the driver in the car.[86]

Jack"Machine Gun" McGurn, Capone's top gunner, was sought as the head trigger man after the massacre.

Moran's men believed they were in the middle of a police bust and lined up facing the brick wall as instructed. That was the last thing they remembered. Shot gun blasts and Thompson machine gun bullets cut down each leaving nothing but a lone howling dog, blood-soaked floor, and seven mutilated bodies.[87] Moran, for whom the bullets were intended, was late arriving at the warehouse that morning and never entered the building, escaping what would have been his sure demise.

While rounding up the usual suspects, officials found Vincenzo Antonio Gibaldi, also known as Jack "Machine Gun" McGurn, Capone's gunner, at the Stevens Hotel registered under the name Vincent D'Oro. Louise Rolfe, an "extravagantly blond lovely," was in his company. They had checked into the hotel two weeks prior and had rarely been seen, meals and newspapers having been sent up. Rolfe would supply McGurn's alibi—they had spent that Valentine's Day in bed until one-thirty. "When you're with Jack, you're never bored," she said.[88]

Implicated as the mastermind, Capone had conveniently spent two hours at the Dade County courthouse being questioned by Robert Taylor, County Solicitor for Dade County, and a King's County, New York, Assistant District Attorney regarding the Yale murder. He was never charged in either incident.[89]

The Genial Host

While Miami residents reeled from news of the massacre, they also experienced Capone's genial side and sincere desire to fit into the sun drenched social scene. Invitations to parties at his house were highly sought after by the wealthy and the affairs were described as "gay, but in perfect taste" and his companions "taciturn but courteous."

Capone's first in a series of bashes had been for sportswriters to publicize the Jack Sharkey-William Stribling fight in February 1929. Prior to the fight, he had visited Sharkey's training camp where he had his photograph taken with the boxer.[90] At the party at 93 Palm Avenue, Capone's hospitable veneer seemed to belie his hard core reputation. He greeted guests with a smile and warm handshake, and was described as a "considerate, somewhat lavish host who . . . had a pronounced desire to forget all about the days back in Cicero."

Frank Getty, a sports writer for United Press who attended one of his press parties, wrote:

Al Capone now is a stout man with coal black hair which is beginning to recede from his wide, sunburned forehead. To watch him moving light-footedly among his guests in his crowded living room, with a word and a smile for everyone and the injunction to "make yourself at home," one loses sight of his background.[91]

Before the Sharkey-Stribling fight held at Flamingo Park in Miami Beach, Capone visited Sharkey's training camp and had his photo taken with the heavyweight champ.

Feeling at Home

An ardent gambler, Capone felt right at home amidst the slot machines, blackjack tables, and dice games that were readily available in illegal gambling houses in Miami Beach or on the mainland in Miami just across the causeway. He also hosted card games at his house where thousands of dollars exchanged hands in the course of an evening.

New York Mirror's nationally syndicated gossip columnist Walter Winchell occasionally visited Capone's Palm Island home. On one such visit while Capone was playing poker with several of his associates, Winchell noted a loaded automatic pistol nearby. He commented to Capone, "I don't' understand that. Here you are playing a game of cards with your friends, but you keep a gun handy." Capone coldly replied, "I have no friends."[92]

After several visits to Capone's home, Winchell wrote that Capone sent him several generous gifts—$16,000 in gambling winnings from roulette and dice tables on Miami Beach, and a greeting card full of winning tickets from a local race track.[93]

Capone Refuses to Budge

Despite the parties, there was growing opposition to Capone's presence. The Outfit's boss, however, wasn't about to give up the Miami lifestyle he so enjoyed without a fight; it just wasn't in his DNA. Even when served a subpoena at his Palm Island estate on February 27, 1929, by a federal grand jury in Chicago, he casually dismissed it, preferring to stay in the Sunshine State.

I have retired, and have moved down here to enjoy myself. I spent the greater part of the year at my place on Palm Island, but it appears I have become a fictional character in the so-called Chicago gang war. Why, if I were only-half as bad as I'm painted, I'd be afraid of myself.[94]

Though his attendance was expected at the hearing slated for March 12, just under two weeks away, Capone took his time in responding. On March 11, one day before his scheduled appearance, he petitioned the court for a postponement claiming that he was too ill to appear. Accompanying his postponement request was a letter from his Miami physician, Dr. Kenneth Phillips, stating that he had been under a doctor's care since January 13, 1929, had pneumonia, and had been confined to bed for six weeks. It further noted that Capone had only been well enough to get out of bed since February 24.

Capone told reporters, "It's on the up and up that I was sick. I came up here when I was able to travel. I don't mind seeing grand juries. I do everything I can to help them. I don't think there'll be anything to this case."[95]

The FBI thought differently and immediately initiated an investigation. It revealed that between January 13 and March 5, 1929, Capone had been seen attending horse races at the Miami Jockey Club in Hialeah. Records also showed that during this time he had taken multiple trips to Nassau and Bimini. On one such charter flight, Capone paid Captain Edward Nirmaier $150 and tipped him another $100 to fly him and several friends to Bimini for a picnic consisting of salami sandwiches and beer. On another trip by steamer, he enjoyed a respite from February 8th through the 12th.

While it was obvious that Capone had been in Miami when the infamous St. Valentine's Day Massacre had occurred, it was equally obvious that Capone was not ill during the weeks in question and was actually in good health.

When he finally appeared in federal court in Chicago, he was cited for contempt and immediately arrested. He posted bail in the amount of $5,000 and was released. Less than two months later on May 17, 1929, Philadelphia authorities, still bent on taking the gangster off the streets, caught up with him outside a movie theater.[96]

The arrest occurred as Capone traveled back from a "peace parley of racket men" in New York. The high-level meeting, the first of its kind and the prequel to forming what became known as "The National Crime Syndicate," was attended by nearly "every important crime figure from the East and Midwest."[97] Having missed their train, Capone, Frank Rio (a.k.a. Frank Cline), and two bodyguards were awaiting a later connection to Chicago when they decided to duck out of sight by taking in a movie. Capone and Rio were nabbed coming out of the theater; the two bodyguards melted into the crowd. Both bearing hand guns, Capone and Rio were charged with carrying a concealed weapon. They were convicted and sentenced to a year in jail with initial time spent in Holmesburg, a county facility in the northeast outskirts of Philadelphia.[98]

Some speculated that Capone actually set up the arrest himself in order to get police protection and out of the lime light for a while after the

St. Valentine's Day Massacre. But, the Outfit's boss was utterly surprised when instead of an obligatory short sentence for a concealed weapons charge he was slapped with a year's stretch in the slammer.

Prison Stay and Release

A curious crowd of hundreds—spectators, photographers, reporters, and supposed gunmen—stood outside the county facility on March 18, 1930, to catch Capone's release at the appointed hour. They were, however, sorely disappointed. Pennsylvania Governor John S. Fisher had secretly released Capone from the Eastern State Penitentiary in Graterford, Pennsylvania, 30 miles away, to where he had been transported just hours earlier. He had served only 10 of his 12-month sentence having received two months off for good behavior.[99] And why not? While other inmates experienced the worst the Pennsylvania penal system could mete out, Capone languished in privilege.

Outfit business was willingly conducted through the warden, and Capone's austere cell was turned into a small but luxurious room complete with antique desk, easy chair, and rug. The *Philadelphia Public Ledger* described Capone's cell: "The whole room was suffused in the glow of a desk lamp which stood on a polished desk . . . On the once-grim walls of the penal chamber hung tasteful paintings, and the strains of a waltz were being emitted by a powerful cabinet radio receiver of handsome design and fine finish . . ."[100]

On the day Capone was released, Herbert Smith, warden of the state pen, stood outside the compound and chided the waiting audience: "What's the use in you people standing around here? We certainly stuck one in your eye that time. The big guy went out from here at 6 o'clock this morning. We shot him away in a brown limousine."[101] While prison officials wouldn't divulge where Capone was headed, it was pretty much assumed he was bound for Florida; after all, Mae and Sonny were already there.

During Capone's imprisonment, Miami had experienced a comfortable respite from the gangster's disruptive presence and that of his hoodlums. With his release, however, that breather was about to be threatened.

CHAPTER 5

MIAMI DOESN'T WANT HIM

I'm out of the booze racket now and I wish the papers would let me alone." [102]

Al Capone

The thought that "Scarface" Capone would return to the Sunshine state was abhorrent to most Floridians. Hope was that authorities would do something to keep him from coming back. The first of those "somethings" happened just before his return. It took the form of a liquor raid at his Palm Island home aimed at finding evidence that would land Capone in jail.

The perfect alibi for the raid had been established weeks earlier in Cincinnati, Ohio, where Roy "Crane Neck" Nugent, a gunner for Capone, had been charged with second-degree-murder involving a bootleg deal gone bad. After the incident, Nugent had flown the coup and landed in Miami. An alert Miami police sergeant had recognized Nugent speeding along the highway with Ralph Capone and two women, all drunk. Nugent told the officer that he was staying at Capone's estate.

Nugent was arrested, but since second degree murder was a bailable offense in Florida at the time, the accused posted a $10,000 bond and was released. When he was about to be picked up by authorities from Ohio, he jumped bail. A Dade County deputy was sent to look for him at

Capone's place, and while Nugent wasn't found, the deputy did note a significant amount of liquor.[103] This event set up the subsequent police raid.

The raid was to be a joint effort by the Dade County Sheriff's Department along with Miami and Miami Beach Police departments. When the Sheriff asked for 20 Miami police officers, however, Miami City Manager Wharton refused: "If there had been a riot, or something of that nature and the sheriff had asked for men, I gladly would have sent all he needed . . . Palm Island is in their [Miami Beach] territory. If they had requested assistance I would have allowed the men to participate in the raid."[104]

Sheriff M.F. Lehman and Miami Beach Police Chief R.H. Wood conducted the search which was authorized by a warrant from Dade County circuit court Judge M.F. Atkinson. The warrant, based upon an affidavit signed by a sheriff's deputy, indicated that the officer had seen liquor in the Capone home several weeks prior when he had gone there to search for Nugent.

Efforts of officers participating in the raid did not go unrewarded. When they carefully opened the door to Capone's second floor locked suite, they found the noted liquor—10 sacks and two bottles of booze—in an adjoining bathroom. In addition to the lavatory booty, they also found a bottle of champagne in the refrigerator and other bottles of booze in a closet near the kitchen.

Heavily armed officers assisting in the raid found Frankie Newton, estate caretaker, at the residence. Officers also located a chef, a maid, and two "negro gardeners."[105] Newton was arrested for liquor possession and vagrancy. Five other men who were swimming at the beach were later arrested when they returned to the island home. All were booked into county jail. Those arrested were John and Albert Capone, brothers of the Chicago Outfit's kingpin; John was arrested for vagrancy and liquor possession and Albert for vagrancy. Louis Cowen, Cicero newspaper publisher, L.J. Brennan of Miami, and Jack McGurn, using the name James Vincent,[106] who were also staying at the estate, were each arrested for vagrancy.

John Capone and Newton posted bond of $500 each; the others $250 each. The Capone brothers denied they knew anything about the liquor and refused to say where their brother Al was, though they indicated he was not in Miami. Newton was allowed to return to the residence, but it was suggested by Judge Atkinson that the other men stay away from the house for the night to avoid complications. They heeded the judge's warning.[107]

Chicago Doesn't Want Him Either

Before heading to Miami, Capone and Rio returned to the Hotel Lexington in Chicago even though they learned that an "arrest on sight" decree had been issued by Chicago police. Bodyguards were stationed in the lobby and at specified posts to alert Capone of police or rival interference. Looking "haggard and not so sleek," the gangland boss spent the better part of the day with Jack Guzick, Frank Nitti, and several of his lieutenants who ran the business while their boss was in jail. Matters at hand included a "review of reports on the beer provinces, refereeing gang disputes, and attending to the thousand and one details required of a high caliber gang chief."

When in Miami Beach, Capone enjoyed swimming in and lounging by his large swimming pool at his 93 Palm Avenue estate.

To Capone's chagrin, reports from the business for the time he was in jail showed a reduction in cash income (at the height of his empire, it is estimated that his income was around $5,000,000 per year). This was attributed to high overhead, the clamping down on Capone's "three big money-making rackets" by Illinois State Attorney John A. Swanson and Chicago Police Commissioner William F. Russel, and his being forced to sign away "many of his rights as 'king' at the Atlantic city 'peace parley.'"[108]

To preempt the arrest on sight pronouncement, Capone , accompanied by his attorney Thomas D. Nash and Phil D'Andrea, apparent city hall "front" for the Capone crowd, calmly walked into the office of Chief of Detectives John Stege and gave himself up. The police were unprepared for such a brash move.

Well dressed in a dark blue suit and tie, white shirt, blue chinchilla overcoat, spats, oxfords, and sporting a bandaged right hand (he had burned it taking a roast out of the oven), Capone, soft spoken and congenial, chatted with newspapermen. He said he had "leisurely motored back to Chicago" and stayed at the home of a friend until he could speak with his attorney. He also told them he had eluded arrest by donning a pair of horn-rimmed glasses (because "the Philadelphia cell ruined my eyes") and passing himself off as a doctor. "And when I registered at a hotel, I just put an M.D. after my name. It worked fine," he said. When asked about the liquor raid at his Miami estate, he said he didn't know anything about it, never kept liquor there, and that the alcohol was not his.

After being shuffled between several offices where, in most cases, no one was in, he was told he was free to go, that there were no arrests pending against him. But he didn't leave without a stern warning from Stege: "What I want you to do is to get out of town and stay out. I'll have my men arrest you every time you appear on the streets as long as you stay here."[109]

George Clarke, reporter for Universal Service, arranged to meet Capone in New York at an undisclosed location to interview him. Clarke described him as a ". . . big man, rotund and muscular; and despite his reputation, he has a friendly face and his is a friendly smile . . . he wore a $100 angora sweater, V-necked, and a white silk shirt open at the throat."

Capone told Clarke how he felt about the concealed weapon arrest:

That was a raw deal if there ever was one. I was carrying a gun. Certainly I was carrying gun. If you got the letters I get from fanatics and cranks, you'd carry a gun too. When I got before Judge Walsh, he socked me with a year. And all of a sudden all of the dirt coming out then in Philadelphia was loaded onto me. I was the goat, but I'm able to take it. But I burned up when they began to take it out on my family. I got a kid brother out to Villa Nova College, near here. He's a nice kid, and was never in any rackets. They caught him driving a car without a license. I don't know, maybe he was coming to see me. Did they give him a break? They did not! They took him downtown to headquarters and called up all the papers.

Capone then showed Clarke a clipping from a New York paper in which the Miami Chamber of Commerce was quoted as imploring the Miami police to position a sign over the "Welcome to Sunnyland" arch at the Miami railroad station. The message to Capone—"Get out and stay out!"

Look at that, and all I ever did for Miami was good! I spent money there, gave money away, and now they want to keep me from my home and family. Well, they can't do it! They're going to try to keep me away. They're going to say "Get out, Capone." Then somebody's going to get hurt—and I'll be blamed for that, too!

All I want is to be left alone . . . If I am not left alone— well, I must protect myself! It's Capone this! Al Capone that! Whenever anyone gets killed, it's 'Al Capone did it.' Why I couldn't have done all the things they say I did in 100 years, and I'm only 31.[110]

Showing His Compassionate Side

Capone's reputation was taking a serious hit with all the negative publicity from gangland murders, public strong arming, and now his stint in prison. To counter that and show the public that he had a compassionate side and was really a kind hearted soul, he opened a soup kitchen in downtown Chicago at 935 South State Street following the start of the Great Depression that, in 1929, had thrown thousands out of work. The first of its kind in the U.S., the kitchen fixed three meals a day and fed hundreds of unemployed men along with women and children.

Unemployed men wait outside a depression soup kitchen opened in Chicago by Al Capone. *Photo courtesy of the U.S. National Archives and Records Administration.*

On occasion, Capone could be seen walking among the men shaking hands, smiling, and offering words of encouragement. The self-serving gesture bolstered the gangster's reputation among the downtrodden who offered toasts to his good health and remarked to papers that, "Capone was doing more for the poor than the entire U.S. government."[111]

Capone Heads for Miami

Once word got out that Capone was headed back to Miami, Goldstrom's Baking Company on Washington Avenue in Miami Beach received an order for a cake, thirty-four inches across, to be delivered to the Palm Island compound.[112] It was presumed the cake was to celebrate Capone's "newfound freedom."[113] But it wasn't just the bakery that would benefit from the mob boss's return. Since merchants and politicians alike had openly solicited Capone's business prior to his incarceration and all seemed to flourish when he and his entourage were in town, the mobster's return would prove yet another opportunity for them to do so.

A week after his release, Capone was featured on the cover of Time magazine. Wearing a tie and business suit with a rose bud pinned to his lapel,[114] the brothel baron's smirk spoke for itself. But Capone's smile would soon fade when he realized that far to his south nobody in the Sunshine State looked forward to his return.

It wasn't just Palm Island residents who objected to Capone being in their community, Dade County's most powerful business and political influences, shared their concern. Among them were: State Attorney Vernon Hawthorne, Miami city commissioners, Miami public safety director S.D. (Sam) McCreary, Miami Beach Chamber of Commerce president Thomas Pancoast, Miami Beach developer Carl G. Fisher, and president of Burdine's, South Florida's largest department store, Roddy B. Burdine.

So concerned were they about Capone's presence in the Miami area, the group unleashed a robust campaign to send Capone packing. Their crusade gained the endorsement of Florida's Governor Doyle Carlton and local newspaper *Miami Daily News*.[115]

The battle was about to begin.

CHAPTER 6

ARREST CAPONE!

They talk about me not being legitimate. Nobody's on the legit. You know that and so do they. Nobody's really on the legit when it comes down to cases.[116]

Al Capone

Pressure to rid the state of this most unwelcomed guest reached all the way to Tallahassee, the state's capital. In a statement to the press, Florida's Governor Doyle E. Carlton declared: "Florida as a playground, in the nature of things, is more liberal than other States, but it will not be a haven to crooks and criminals or headquarters for gangsters and gunmen. He [Capone] may for a time wrap about himself the technicalities of the law, other criminals have. He may for a time. He will not establish headquarters in Florida. His element will not take root here. His attendants will not be an armed guard to protect him in his past crimes against society."[117]

So repugnant was the possibility that Capone would return to take up permanent residency that on March 19, 1930, while the governor was in Jacksonville to attend Governor's Day at the Florida State Fair, he drafted a telegram in his hotel room directed to all Florida law enforcement officials. It read: "It is reported that Al Capone is on his way to Florida.

Arrest promptly if he comes your way and escort him to the state border. He cannot remain in Florida. If you need additional assistance, call me."[118] His message was loud and clear.

Sheriffs on the Lookout, Threatened

Sherriff's deputies throughout the state were ordered to be on the lookout for Capone. W.B. Cahoon, sheriff of Duval County, who believed he might show up at the Jacksonville Municipal Airport, weighed in on what he intended to do should the gangster come through his jurisdiction: "Capone has no visible means of support and we'll clap him into jail as a vagrant."

On Palm Island, Miami Beach officers were stationed at the entrance where they peered into cars at passengers hoping to find the gangland king. While several of Capone's men were recognized, to the officer's chagrin Capone was not among them. At his residence, a swarm of activity was taking place as autos and delivery trucks came and went at all hours in preparation for his return.

In Broward County, Just north of Miami, Sheriff A.W. Turner received a threatening letter from Don Collins, one of Capone's alleged aids who served him both in Chicago and Miami. Having been arrested by Sheriff Deputies for breaking and entering, Collins was being held at the Broward County jail when the threat arrived. It was printed in ink on stationery from the Savoy hotel in Miami.

Collins, a.k.a. Blowser Walsh, Kinkaid Kid, and John Leeger, had handed a note to Dot McKinnon (of Miami and Chicago) a couple of days prior and asked that she deliver it to the Capones or their associates in Miami, telling her they would finance his release. The note was intercepted.

The subsequent threat which read, "Spring Dan Collins and A. Pond (his pal) before Saturday night or take the consequences," was signed with two crosses. In addition to the threat, officers at the jail discovered hacksaw blades in Pond's mattress. They believed the find thwarted Collins's jail break.[119]

Governor's Decree Sparks Reaction from Across the Nation

As soon as the governor's decree to arrest Capone should he set foot in Florida hit newspapers, word spread nationally. Shortly thereafter, the Governor received hundreds of letters from residents of Florida and states further north congratulating him for taking a definitive stand against Capone.

A letter from Joel Johnston of Charlevoix, Michigan, stated:

I certainly want to congradulate [sic] you on your noble stand against that low down degenerate Capone. I am disgusted with the newspapers giving him so much front page notice. It only encourages him and others to do likewise, and it is a dam [sic] shame for Chicago officers to know him so well and yet say that they have no charge against him, I think the answer is (money) . . .[120]

Another letter from H. Marsh of Parkersburg, West Virginia, also showed support for the Governor: ". . . Your pronouncements are, I believe, the first sensible expressions we have ever seen in the press anywhere concerning Al Capone and his ilk . . ."[121] So did a letter from attorney Angus Sumner from Fort Pierce, Florida: "I want to congratulate you on the stand you have taken on the Al Capone matter, and let you know that the people of this community are behind you in keeping him out of this state."[122] Even the First Baptist Church in Punta Gorda, Florida, endorsed the governor's declaration against Capone.[123]

One of the most colorful letters was written by Clarence E. Woods of Champaign County, Illinois, to Miami Beach judge Frank A. Katzenbine:

I write to extend congratulations to you for your treatment of this noted individual (Capone) who has succeeded in attaining eminence hardly second to that of the President of the Chamber of Commerce of Chicago, Isham Randolph, who is spending thousands of dollars running around over the Southern and Southwestern States with a special train of boosters trying to create "Good Will and Confidence in Chicago" as a counter-irritant for the foul reputation which the Capones and their ilk have given the Windy City by the Unsalted Sea.

The greatest aid you could bestow upon Chicago would be to feed Al and his gang to the zoological sharks down there, and wire Dr. Randolph to return home, that they will be safe now since you have caponized Capone and his satellites.[124]

66

But ridding Florida of Capone wasn't as easy as the governor thought. The Chicago crime boss was bent on staying in his Miami Beach home and nothing save death was going to pry him loose.

Hiring Legal Representation

In order for Capone to fight the governor, Palm Island citizens, and law enforcement agencies from routing him from Florida, he needed savvy legal representation. He found that in not one, but two Florida attorneys— Vincent Claude Giblin and James Francis "Fritz" Gordon.

Giblin had grown up in Mobile Alabama. With both parents having died before he was fourteen, he was left an orphan. An obviously bright young man, he finished high school and went on to attend Notre Dame's law school on scholarship without having ever attended undergraduate school. He graduated in 1918. After moving to Florida, Giblin practiced law for the next nine years in Escambia, Duval, and Broward counties. He became Broward County's first circuit judge in 1927 by appointment of Governor John W. Martin "over the objections of the local Ku Klux Klan to a Roman Catholic filling the post." Two years later, Giblin moved to Miami and opened a private practice.[125] It was there he became associated with Gordon.

Gordon, also from the South, was a Georgia Cracker from Griffin, Georgia, and attended Mercer University School of Law in Macon, Georgia. In 1925, he was admitted to the Florida bar and spent his first year serving as trust officer for the Commercial Bank & Trust Company of Miami. For the next two years, Gordon prosecuted criminal cases as Assistant Solicitor for Dade County.[126]

It is unknown why Capone decided to engage the services of Giblin and Gordon or why the highly reputable attorneys agreed to represent the Chicago mobster who had earned such a nefarious reputation. Perhaps it was the money, the notoriety such representation might bring, or maybe it was simply the challenge of it all. Whatever the reason, in 1930, Giblin, 32, and Gordon, 27, accepted Capone as a client and filed suit in federal court in Miami to stop Florida's sheriffs from obstructing their client's attempt to reoccupy his Palm Island residence.

Capone had always maintained that he'd done nothing but bring business to the area and that now all he wanted to do was live in Miami free from police harassment. Apparently, Judge Halstead R. Ritter agreed.

Six days later he issued a temporary restraining order that blocked the governor's efforts to oust Capone. The order enjoined the sheriffs from:

> . . . *seizing, arresting, kidnapping or abducting the plaintiff, Alphonse Capone, without warrant or authority of law; from transporting, banishing or expelling the said plaintiff from the state of Florida without warrant or authority of law, and from molesting, annoying or interfering with the said plaintiff in entering the state of Florida and proceeding to his home in Dade county, state of Florida under penalty of being adjudged in contempt of this court for violation of this order.*[127]

Sheriffs in each of the twenty counties through which Capone would likely travel were served copies of the injunction by Giblin.[128]

"Machine Gun" McGurn Arrested

While Capone was in Chicago getting his affairs in order for his eventual return to Florida, Jack McGurn and "a pretty blond woman," both tournament-level golfers,[129] set out from Capone's Palm Island estate with McGurn's brother Tony[130] to enjoy a round of golf on a Miami Beach golf course. Their amusement was cut short on the fifth hole, however, when Chief Deputy Sheriff D.C. Coleman and another officer approached the threesome.

After telling Jack that a fugitive warrant had been issued for his arrest by Chicago authorities for jumping a $10,000 bond in connection with a charge of carrying a concealed weapon, the attending officer frisked the gangland gunner. When no gun was found, Jack brazenly asked the officers if the group could finish their putts. Amazingly, they agreed.

Jack took his time lining up the eight-foot putt, but his efforts went unrewarded when the ball slid past the hole. After sinking his second putt, Jack nodded to the officers—he was now ready to accompany them to police headquarters.

At the station, the blond was allowed to go free. Capone's attorney Fritz Gordon announced he would seek habeas corpus release for the McGurn brothers. Tony was later released, but following a futile attempt to get bond for Jack, Gordon said no further steps would be taken; they would await extradition papers from Chicago.

The blond, it was intimated, may have been Louise Rolfe, the same woman who supplied McGurn's alibi after the St. Valentine's Day massacre. That woman, who was known in Chicago as "the Blond Alibi," was the same one who had been with McGurn when he was sought as the massacre's trigger man.[131] McGurn and Rolfe later married to avoid her testifying against him in court.[132]

Jack "Machine Gun" McGurn, Capone's top gunner, was a tournament-level golfer who enjoyed playing on Miami Beach golf courses when in town.

Capone Arrives in South Florida

On Sunday morning, April 20, 1930, while forty thousand gathered on Miami Beach for Easter Sunrise Services, a train carrying Capone, his thirteen-year-old nephew Ralph Jr., former Chicago alderman Albert J. Prignano, and numerous bodyguards pulled into the Florida East Coast Railway station in Hollywood, Florida, just north of Miami. Meeting the train, which let off Florida's foremost persona non grata, were more bodyguards and three bullet-proof limousines.[133]

The bodyguards were described as resembling "military combat guards" who marched "ahead, behind and across the street, when he [Capone] goes on foot through Chicago streets." His super-armed automobiles were: "The latest type of a racer had the staunchness of a battleship—in prospect of offense or defense in ramming operations—and the windows in the steel sides are made of the so-called 'bullet-proof' glass, which will not really resist a bullet, but will not splinter when struck. In the front, in the interior of the car, are submachine, rifle and short-barreled shot-guns and ammunition boxes. Similar armament rests over the back seat. Under the windshield and in front and along the edge of the window at the back are narrow steel shutter flaps through which rifles and shotguns may be thrust."

On April 21, the *Miami Daily News* covered Capone's arrival in Hollywood. Alongside that article, it reprinted a story by rival newspaper *Miami Herald* that reported something quite different from that of the *News*. The *Herald's* story, which the *Miami Daily News* said appeared to be an account "officially authorized" by Capone, noted that the mob boss and his nephew were greeted by attorneys Giblin and Gordon when they arrived by train in Miami. In actuality, the entourage had disembarked in Hollywood and driven to Miami.

The *Herald* article went on to note that one of its reporters had interviewed Capone later that day at his home on Palm Island and told readers the mob boss had entertained his son and nephew by taking them for a speedboat ride on Biscayne Bay.

A man traveling south aboard the Dixie Limited who unexpectedly found himself a fellow passenger of the Chicago gangster told the *Miami Daily News* that Capone's hoodlums, "moved in and out of their chief's drawing room almost continuously, that a poker game was in progress much of the time accompanied by loud talk that was mostly profanity, and that other passengers in the area were thoroughly frightened." He also described how uniformed attendants rushed around carrying baskets of cracked ice and mixer bottles of ginger ale, each waiter trying to out-hustle the other in anticipation of large tips.[134]

Miami Daily News Spearheads Ousting Campaign

The *Miami Daily News*, part of the Cox newspaper chain owned by the former Ohio governor James M. Cox, 1920 Democratic Party nominee for president, and a Florida "snowbird," was an ardent critic of Capone. With his son-in-law Daniel J. Mahoney at the helm of the publication as general manager, the paper supplied daily sustenance to thirsty readers by reporting Capone's every move. Articles and edgy front page editorials kept citizens informed, and if they lured readers from rival newspaper *Miami Herald,* whom they believed was treating Capone with kid gloves, then so be it.

Constantly referring to the mob head as "Scarface Al Capone, alias A. Acosta, alias Al Brown," they ran a string of editorials geared at defaming the gangster. One such editorial noted: ". . . There is no surprise in Capone's defying the spiritual sense of the people of Florida. He laughs at law, he gives it no respect; through the organized forms of criminal operation he has with one exception escaped, up until this day, anything beyond arrest or detention upon suspicion. . ."

Cox and Mahoney were among those from the Miami Area who had entreated Governor Carlton to stop Capone at the Florida border. With the governor having no legal reason to keep him out, however, Cox and Mahoney had embarked upon their editorial campaign with gusto. After several days of inflammatory articles, Mahoney said phone calls came in wondering if he would like to be "measured for a coffin." His response was swift: "I would like to meet at any hour at any place the man who thinks he's big enough to put me in it!"

The tension between Capone and Cox didn't end there. At a party one night, Cox discovered that Capone was also a guest. The newspaper owner demanded that the "bum" leave or he would. The host, no doubt red-faced and with a large lump in his throat, asked Capone to leave.[135]

Cox later wrote in his autobiography *Journey Through My Years* that one day while in his office a visitor made a very unusual visit. The man, who was very stylishly dressed, walked into Cox's office and laid down a certified check in the amount of $500,000. He told Cox it represented the first payment from an anonymous client who wanted to purchase the paper for $5,000,000 in cash. Cox refused the offer. "The property was not worth that amount at that time, and there was not the slightest doubt in my mind that the Capone interests were behind the offer," wrote Cox.[136] When the man asked how much it could cost to purchase the newspaper, Cox is said to have replied, "Five cents, on any street corner."[137]

The *Miami Daily News* continued to run front-page editorials that denounced the mobster's arrival and greater Miami's "indifference" to his presence. In one editorial, the paper accused casinos in Miami and Miami Beach of being "directly under the thumb" of the gangster. The article also chastised citizens for being spellbound by the lure of Capone's generous spending sprees and turning a blind eye to his presence: "A man with criminal associations, with a record known world-wide of defiance of law and public decency, is fast puncturing the very pith and fiber of our whole set-up here. The power of money is known. There is nothing more persuasive, either for good or evil, than gold, and Greater Miami in her indifference has established here one of the most dangerous characters on earth, with all the power of a feudal lord."[138]

Feudal lord, perhaps, but it was no secret that Miami and Miami Beach had been operating as a hotbed of illegal gambling, prostitution, corruption, and rum running long before Capone entered the scene.

Miami's Not So Pristine Past

Henry Flagler introduced gambling to the state when he built his "high-toned gambling houses along with his hotels. Thus St. Augustine had its Bacchus club, Palm Beach a Beach Club . . . and Miami had a Seminole Club tucked away . . . next to the Royal Palm Hotel." Only tourists were allowed inside as they were considered "respectable, necessary parts of a rich man's resort . . ."

From these beginnings, gambling permeated the very fabric of Miami and Miami Beach. Soon, the poor accompanied the rich in being enticed by the opportunity to get rich quick. So much so, that by 1929, gambling had become a way of life even though it was illegal. Locals, many of whom were city officials and high profile businessmen, ran these enterprises making their own "arrangements with the sheriff and city police and through small-town consensus . . ."[139]

But it wasn't just gambling. Many of these same individuals made cat houses and illegal booze part of their business plan long before Capone came to town. Correspondence to and from Carl Fisher indicate "a constant movement of liquor and beer between Carl and his friends as early as 1921, including instructions on how to avoid detection. The illegal booze and beer network included newspaper publisher Cox."[140]

Could it be all the hoopla over Capone's presence was because the Greater Miami's good-ole-boy business-as-usual network had become threatened? After all, when Michael Glenn, security manager for Carl Fisher was asked to "watch" Capone, he reported back:

> . . . The [Palm] Island Club opened this past winter January 15th under a new management and Capone has one-fourth interest for which he paid $25,000 to the present owners. He also had a one-fourth interest in the Floridian Hotel gambling room in which he installed crooked gambling devices. He had two Chicago gunmen stationed in this room at $40.00 a night to protect it from any outside interference. He also owns the controlling interest in the South Beach dog track, and Carter's gambling house, as well as Albert Bouche's Villa Venice. He tried to muscle in at the Deauville Casino, but was refused, and after some kind of a threat, some men were brought from New York to protect [the] Deauville from Capone's crowd . . . [141]

Yet Capone's enterprises weren't the only discoveries. The report went on to note that one night a local gambling house was raided by private detectives who removed all the gaming devices. Word soon reached the Sheriff's office that if the gambling machines were not brought back by the following day somebody would land in jail. Apparently the proprietor was paying $1,000 a week for protection and he "would not stand for a double cross." All the machines were returned the next day.

In another incident, 300 cases of whiskey were hijacked from a bootlegger by the Sheriff's office and taken to Hialeah. The savvy bootlegger located the stash and went to retrieve it. While he and his men were loading it into trucks, the Hialeah police arrived. They placed all the men under arrest, confiscated the liquor, and transported it to the Hialeah police station. The Sheriff's office showed up later, appropriated 100 cases, and turned around and sold the liquor to a hotel in Coral Gables. While the incident was reported to Prohibition officials, no arrests were ever made. Somebody had bought them off.

Glenn concluded his report with the following: "The above incidents will show you the futility of trying to rid the community of a man like Capone, with our present City and County officials."[142]

Carl Graham Fisher, developer of Miami Beach, joined efforts to oust Capone despite his own indulgence into the illegal booze business. *(ca. 1916) Photo courtesy State Archives of Florida, Florida Memory, Gleason Waite Romer photographer.*

Hope for Peace and Quiet

In contrast to what officials knew to be true, Capone told a *Miami Herald* reporter: "I have no interest in politics, neither in Chicago nor Miami. I am here for rest, which I think I deserve. All I want is a fair break. I have done nothing in violation of the law in Miami and will not. All I ask is to be left alone and enjoy the home I have purchased here."[143]

While that may have been for what the Chicago gangster had hoped, Miami residents didn't believe one word. And they weren't about to let the new resident relax. Multiple arrests on a variety of charges were just around the corner.

CHAPTER 7

NO REST FOR THE WEARY

*I'm the boss. I'm going to continue to run things. They've
been putting the roscoe on me for a good many years and I'm
still healthy and happy. Don't let anybody kid you into
thinking I can be run out of town. I haven't run yet and I'm
not going to.*[144]

Al Capone

On April 25, 1930, Judge Halstead Ritter announced that his
temporary injunction banning the harassment of Capone was now
permanent. This meant that the twenty sheriffs who had received
the initial injunction were forever prohibited from ousting the infamous
mobster.[145] In response, Governor Carlton put out a press release:

*I make no apology for and no retreat from my original
stand. Florida as a playground, in the nature of things is
more liberal than some other states. It will not, however,
be a haven for crooks and criminals or the headquarters
for gangsters and gunmen . . . Capone is the recognized
leader of perhaps the most vicious gang that ever infested
a city, a gang to whom the constitution and the law mean
nothing when it is to protect property and life of the other
fellow. So far as I am concerned he is an outlaw and those*

*who wish to court and fondle and make him a hero can
assume full responsibility for their actions. . .*[146]

About the same time Ritter was making his declaration, a Dade
County grand jury was taking its war on Capone to the front line.

Authorities Seek to Padlock 93 Palm Avenue

Two days after Capone arrived in Miami, the first in a series of
legal actions was delivered to 93 Palm Avenue with the intention of
forcing the Chicago mobster to vacate the area. The suit, filed by Dade
County State Attorney N. Vernon Hawthorne, sought to padlock Capone's
home on grounds that it was a "public nuisance." In support of the
allegation, Hawthorne claimed that Capone's house had been used as a
"retreat for all classes of criminals, racketeers and fugitives from justice,"
that illegal liquor had been "kept and served" on the property, and that
Capone's presence had negatively impacted property values.

Grand jury members threw their support behind Hawthorne's
padlock suit stating: "We endorse, commend and urge all legitimate efforts
to exterminate from the community what clearly appears to be a cancerous
growth of organized crime." To further emphasize their commitment,
Miami Beach assigned two officers to keep close tabs on Capone and his
residence 24 hours a day and to document all movement.[147]

While waiting for the case to come to trial, Capone boarded a
plane at Dinner Key in Miami and headed for Havana, Cuba.
Accompanying him were attorney Fritz Gordon, banker Albert J.
Prepeano, strong-arm aid Sylvie Agoglia, Chicago *American* editor Harry
Read, salesman Nicholas Carew, and Dr. A.J. Bertram, a Miami physician.

Upon arrival in the island capital, Capone was called before the
chief of the national secret services, Santiago Trujillo Martinez, who
queried him as to the purpose of his trip. After Capone assured the chief
that he was merely a retired businessman from Chicago and only there for
pleasure, Martinez released him and said they planned no action against
him so long as he behaved himself.

After checking into his hotel, a suite on the third floor of the
Sevilla-Biltmore, Capone immediately called upon the skills of the hotel
barber and manicurist, tossing them $5 gold pieces for their services.
Waiters and bell boys servicing the gang lord received generous tips as
well.[148]

Several days into his trip, Capone hosted a dinner in an extravagantly appointed dining room for a number of leading residents, including Captain Arvara Nesperiera, the mayor's representative. It was rumored Capone's visit was to purchase "valuable liquors" from the American financed Elcano distillery store then involved in bankruptcy proceedings.[149] Associated Press reports from the Cuban capital, however, relayed to readers something quite different. They stated that Capone's reason for the trip was to "establish a temporary residence there, seeking relief from the repeated reminders at Miami that he and his gang are not wanted there."[150]

Al Capone (middle), leaves Tropical Garden restaurant in Havana, Cuba, with his attorney J. Fritz Gordon (left), and Mayor of Havana, Julio Morales (right). *Photo courtesy of State Archives of Florida.*

Capone's current trip appeared quite different from one he took to Havana in 1928. During that trip, which only lasted a few days, he opened a pool room in the Almendares district of Marianao, an exclusive residential neighborhood. Several partners in the venture tried to carry on the business after Capone returned to Florida, but harassment by Cuba's secret police proved too taxing for the establishment's customers. It closed shortly thereafter. Capone later declared that Cuba offered no "field for this particular kind of business."[151]

Once he arrived back in Florida, Chicago's head gangster awaited trial in the padlock case by loafing around his Palm Island estate. He played cards, swam, and went fishing off his boat. One day while in the Gulfstream, he caught a 70-pound sailfish almost eight feet long. It was among one of the largest hooked that season.[152]

At the same time Capone was enjoying the amenities of South Florida, back in Chicago 25 members of his gang were busted for producing whiskey—400,000 gallons within a two and a half year period. Assistant U.S. District Attorney Daniel Anderson told reporters that at the center of the investigation was the Italian Importing and Manufacturing Company. Capone's men—Charles Argento, Joseph Almanza, and Frank Barone—had taken it over in November 1927 and run it as part of Capone's empire; all were indicted. According to Anderson, corn sugar in 100 carload lots had been distributed by the company to stills sprinkled throughout Illinois and Wisconsin.[153]

Golf Course Hosts Entourage

In addition to playing cards, taking his boat *Arrow* out on the bay, fishing, or playing tennis, several times a week, Capone and his entourage could be found on the Miami Beach municipal golf course. Many times his gang played without him.

The men were "lavish spenders," tipping their caddies and helpful staff quite generously. Buying golf balls by the box, they used them on the practice range and if while playing golf one of the gang hit a ball out of bounds, they never searched for it.

Having experienced the power of safety in numbers, Capone's gang preferred to play in one group of seven or eight. Course staff, however, was finally able to convince them to break up into the customary foursomes. Using assumed names, Capone's men enjoyed their time on the course with locals none the wiser that they were sharing fairways with Chicago's infamous thugs. That anonymity came to an abrupt end, however, when an unsuspecting foursome witnessed a most unusual event.

It began as an innocuous occurrence—a car filled with men driving along the road adjacent to the golf course. When the car came to a stop at the fifth green, however, the scene quickly changed. Capone's men, who were just lining up their putts, immediately dropped their putters, grabbed their golf bags, and dove into a bunker. Their corporate means of defense—sawed-off shotguns—were quickly pulled from their bags.

While there was no attack, the jig was up and proved too much for several of the caddies. They resigned their posts right then and there.[154]

Capone's Double

Stories about Capone's liquor smuggling, raids, and arrests were abundant in newspapers from New York to Miami, yet some levity was brought to bear when fifteen detectives and newspaper reporters along with cameramen and spectators gathered at the Brooklyn pier to meet the *Toloa*, a steamer just concluding its voyage from Havana to New York. The crowd was expecting to see the Chicago gang lord himself who was rumored to be aboard. When the ship docked, however, it was Anthony Perrapato, mayor of Garfield, New Jersey, that strolled down the gangway. Perrapato remarked that fellow passengers had "pointed him out as curiosity" the entire trip.[155]

Anthony Parrapato (l), mayor of Garfield, New Jersey (1928-1934), was mistaken for Al Capone (r). *Photo courtesy of Howard Lanza, Garfield Historical Society.*

Judge Hears Arguments in Padlock Case

The first day of the padlock case arrived. Capone, fashionably dressed in a brown suit, brown socks, and terra cotta tie, sat in the courtroom next to attorneys Giblin and Gordon flashing a "half-smile, half-leer, which never left his face," and "a diamond as big as a serpent's egg on his left hand." Accompanying him were his wife Mae, who was modestly dressed in a "black and white ensemble and a large white fur neckpiece," his brother Albert, and Sonny.

State Attorney Hawthorne contended that the nuisance charge stemmed from the fact that liquor was stored in Capone's Palm Island residence and that the dwelling had been a harbor for "criminals and the criminal element" bringing embarrassment to the community and harming its reputation.

A packed courtroom heard Giblin argue that the arrest was not in keeping with the criminal acts with which Capone was charged:

> It must be shown that liquor was being stored in the house at the time the complaint was filed if this is to be used as evidence of nuisance. It is not enough to say that liquor has been stored there many times. Neither is it enough to charge that criminals are harbored there. If these men have paid the penalty for their wrong-doing, there is no offense in sheltering them.

He also reminded the court that his client wasn't even in town when the raid was conducted and the arrests made. To that, Hawthorne retorted: "It is no crime to allow a rattlesnake to live, but if you allow one to roam loose in your yard, where it may bite children and other persons, any court in the world will declare it a nuisance and authorize steps to abate it."

After extended argument on both sides, Judge Paul D. Barns deferred the case until the following week. When court adjourned, throngs of well-wishers patted Capone on the back and shook his hand. He responded with laughs and jokes.

Just outside the courtroom, dozens of curious spectators assembled in the hallway to get a glimpse of the infamous brothel, liquor, and gambling king as he emerged. Gordon and Capone, however, slipped out a back door and down the stairs unseen.[156]

Real Estate Agent Tries to Bribe Judge?

While Capone's padlock case was being considered by Judge Barns, Nathan Grebstein, a real estate agent, sat in a local jail on a contempt of court charge. Barns brought the charge against Grebstein when, on two occasions, the arrested man offered the judge $5,000 to rule in favor of Capone. The first time Grebstein made the offer, Barns dismissed his advance as a misguided act. When Grebstein approached the judge again the next day, however, all bets were off. Barns ordered the realtor's arrest.

In State Supreme Court where Grebstein filed his answer in connection with habeas corpus proceedings brought about by his attorney M.H. Rosenhouse, the realtor's version of the incident proved decidedly different to that of the judge's. According to Grebstein, after the first hearing, in which he sat inside the rail, an area reserved for attorneys, he was on his way out of court when he was approached by an unknown person who believed he had certain influence with the court. It was this person, the realtor said, that told him $5,000 was available to the judge if he ruled "a certain way." Being the good citizen that he was, Grebstein went to the judge to tell him what had transpired. The realtor maintained that his only goal was to protect the court from gossip.[157]

After the case went up to the Florida Supreme court and was returned to Judge Barns, he released Grebstein for time served, and referred to him, "as much a fool as a knave. . ."[158]

Theater Invitation Results in Inadvertent Arrest

Capone was home awaiting continuation of the padlock case when, on May 8, the manager of the Olympia Theater in downtown Miami phoned to invite him to a movie. The matinee, the newly released *The Return of Dr. Fu Manchu*, was the second film in a series about the evil Asian criminal genius.[159] Accompanied by his brother John, former Chicago Alderman Albert J. Prignano, and bodyguard Nick Circella, none of them armed, Capone headed across the County Causeway (now MacArthur Causeway) from Miami Beach to Miami. They didn't get far. Upon entering the mainland, they were stopped by two detectives who had been dispatched by Miami police chief, Guy C. Reeve. The chief had been given the directive, "Arrest Capone on sight," by Sam McCreary, Miami's director of public safety.

The men were taken to the police station where, without just cause, they were searched, fingerprinted, photographed, and booked.[160] Denied a phone call to his attorney, receipt for his valuables—gold jewelry and cash of $1,160—or food and water (a pitcher of ice water was later brought to the cell), Capone was placed separately in an interior cell. After some time, McCreary visited Capone to give him the unwelcomed news—he would be arrested "anytime, anywhere, in any company, every time he set foot within the jurisdiction of the city of Miami." Capone asked if this meant even if his wife and son were with him. McCreary answered in the affirmative.[161]

Attorneys Giblin and Gordon charged into the station within an hour of the arrest after having been alerted by someone who had witnessed Capone's nabbing by police. Gordon and McCreary got into a heated verbal argument that morphed into a physical shoving match when the lawyer was told that all visitors to see Capone, including his attorneys, would be searched. The scuffle ended when Gordon fled the station with several officers in pursuit. When officers caught up with the attorney a half block later, he was restrained and forcibly searched. They found no weapon.

In judge's chambers where the hearing took place, city commissioners, policemen, detectives, and citizens packed the room, rendering it most stifling. John Capone, "groggy and bleary-eyed," appeared to be suffering from lack of sleep. Even brother Al was not his usual coiffured self. All sat coatless, wiping perspiration from their faces.

After hearing both attorneys, Judge Uly O. Thompson rendered his decision:

> *The court takes cognizance form its own records as to the presence of one of the defendants, Al Capone, in whose connection proceedings already have been begun in another division of this court to have his home declared a public nuisance. Under the showing made her, however, that no warrants have been issued, the defendants will be ordered discharged in this case.*[162]

Mobster's Thugs Attack Citizens

On the heels of Capone's second arrest, Frank H. Wharton, city manager, was warned to "get out of town." Albert P. Hinson, Wharton's brother-in-law, relayed the warning when he announced to police that two unidentified men, whom he believed were Capone's gangsters, had assaulted him.

Bleeding from a wound just behind his left ear, Wharton walked into the county jail around 11:00 p.m. and told officers that he was on his way to catch a street car to Miami Beach when two men got out of a large sedan, knocked him to the ground, and dazed him. They then cursed him before leveling the hissed warning against his brother-in-law. Hinson requested police presence to guard Wharton's house because he was afraid his brother-in-law might be killed because of his active efforts to rid Miami of Capone.[163]

Capone Arrested . . . Again

Five nights after Capone's arrest at the causeway, he was sitting in his box at the American Legion hall awaiting the fights which would headline the lightweight "Dixie Championship" between boxers Joe "Kid" Peck and Jimmy Spivey. The enjoyment was short lived. Before he witnessed even one fight, a detective tapped Capone on the shoulder and told him Chief Reeve was in the back of the hall and wanted to see him. He was under arrest again, along with companions Sylvestor Agoglia, who gave his occupation as Capone's "undertaker," Albert Prignano, former Chicago alderman, and Nick Circella who claimed he was a "fight manager."

The action was a surprise to both Capone and Giblin, who happened to be sitting next to his client, since judge's orders given City Manager Frank Wharton stated that Capone was not be molested unless he violated a law or a warrant was obtained. Unable to spring Capone and his men because a judge wasn't available to issue writs of habeas corpus to determine if the detention was valid, all Giblin could do was wait out his client's 17-hour incarceration.

The next day, Miami Mayor C.H. Reeder, director of public safety Sam McCreary, City Manager F.H. Warton, and Chief Reeve testified before Judge Thompson. McCreary said he had ordered the arrest after consulting Wharton and two city commissioners because he had received innumerable complaints from the "best business people" that Capone "menaced society and reduced Miami's citizens to fear."

When asked about city policy, Reeder stated that the commission had given him instructions to arrest Capone every time he was in Miami and added that he considered Capone's presence a "greater menace than an epidemic or a hurricane."

In making his decision to release all four prisoners, Judge Thompson said that he did not take the position a warrant always must be issued before an arrest could be make, or that the arresting officers must see a crime committed. He merely held that the city had made no showing legally sufficient to hold the men.[164]

Al Capone (l) is escorted by Miami police officers Detective Jester, Chief of Police Guy Reeve, and Detective John McClendon. *Photo courtesy of History Miami.*

More Troubles in Illinois

While Capone remained enveloped in myriad arrests and legal issues in Miami, Chicago authorities were doing their best to rid their area of the gang lord. On May 8, 1930, Federal prohibition agents raided the Cotton Club and the Greyhound Inn, both Cicero clubs owned by Capone and managed by his brother Ralph, in hopes of finding connections to vigorous beer traffic in Cicero. Arrested were bartenders and waiters while fashionably dressed women and men, who were neither questioned nor arrested, looked on. Ralph Capone, who managed the club, was not found.

The next day, feds announced that the previous night's raid, part of an on-going investigation into whiskey smuggling by air, had uncovered an airline whose high speed planes had dropped more than $1,000,000 worth of Canadian whiskey into Chicago during an eight month period. Two planes valued at $60,000 were allegedly used in the operation that included round trips between Windsor, Ontario, and Chicago six days a week. The planes were believed to have made 200 flights bringing in 14,000 cases of liquor worth a whopping $1,400,000. Ralph Capone was later arrested, arraigned, and released under $5,000 bond.[165]

Through information obtained from the raid on the Cotton Club, Federal Prohibition agents confiscated 18,000 pints of illegal whiskey worth $75,000 from a rail car labeled "Lumber." The liquor, G&W bourbon, as well as Indian Hill and Old Crow whiskies, were originally distilled in the U.S. They had been exported to Canada, rebottled and stamped, and sent to Bimini. The booze had subsequently been smuggled into Florida and placed on a rail car in Jacksonville for shipment to Chicago. The elaborate repackaging and routing system was designed to confuse authorities and deflect suspicion.

The rail car was registered under the name of Racine Lumber Company; however, authorities could not locate a lumber company under that name. For two days the car sat on the Illinois Central siding until orders were received from Florida to transfer the car to the Baltimore and Ohio yards. Transfer was prevented by the seizure.[166]

Vagrancy Law Leads to Second Arrest at the Fights

More trouble awaited Capone in Miami. To add teeth to the existing city pickup law, on May 15, the Miami city council members passed a new vagrancy law—one that would include conditions under which Capone and his associates would be more vulnerable. The ordinance included several provisions for pickup including: "'persons having visible means of support acquired by unlawful or illegal means or methods,' those 'dangerous to public safety or peace of the city of Miami,' and those 'known or reputed to be crooks, gangsters or hijackers.'"[167] The violation came with a penalty of $500 or imprisonment of up to 60 days or both.[168]

On the night of May 19, Capone was arrested once again while at the fights, this time for vagrancy. He was out in short order after posting $100 bond. At hearings two days later, Giblin asked for dismissal of charges since the warrants charged the pair with "wandering from place to place without lawful business while the state statute is worded 'without lawful object or purpose.'" He also stated that the wording of the warrant said Capone was "an idle and dissolute person," while the statute actually included the words, "who goes about begging." Giblin added that there was no law that forced a person to have gainful employment. As far as Prignano, he was arrested simply because he was an "associate" of Capone. To associate with a criminal, argued Giblin, is not against the law.

In the end, the case was dismissed. Ironically, just before Capone's case, the judge had heard charges of vagrancy against four youths. Appearing without representation, the youths had received 30 days in jail.[169]

CHAPTER 8

TRIALS CONTINUE

"When I sell liquor, it's called bootlegging; when my patrons serve it on Lake Shore Drive, it's called hospitality."[170]

Al Capone

Just days after Capone was arrested on vagrancy charges, police stopped him for the fourth time while he was on his way to his attorneys' office. Giblin told his client not to go along with the officers unless he felt obliged to do so. Capone refused to accompany city detective C.F. Potterton and the other officer, so they left.[171] To Capone, the incident was the last straw. He brought charges of conspiracy against the mayor, Commissioner John Knight, Sam McCreary, and Jim Cox. To charges against McCreary, he added a second one—false imprisonment.

Justice of the Peace Warren L. Newcomb presided over the preliminary hearing to determine if there was enough evidence to go to trial. After hearing testimony, the judge dismissed the conspiracy charges outright but adjourned to consider the charge of false imprisonment against McCreary. He also told the police that if they bothered Capone while he was under subpoena as a prosecution witness, he would have them arrested. Acquiescing to the judgement of the court, McCreary announced that Capone would no longer be arrested on sight.[172]

Spectators Pack Courtroom in Padlock Case

Finally, the padlock case went to trial. More than one hundred spectators packed the courtroom to see Scarface Capone and hear the testimony of 50 witnesses, 13 lined up for the defense. Carl Fisher, developer of Miami Beach, was to be the first of the state's 40 witnesses to testify. The *Miami Daily News* described Capone as ". . . leering at the pioneer Beach developer with fixed gaze." Fisher reportedly leered back.

Crowd expectations of hearing testimony turned to frustration when arrangements were made for Fisher to testify in the judge's chamber. The *News* later obtained the transcript of the businessman's testimony and printed it in the paper.

Testifying for the prosecution, Fisher reiterated his assertion that Capone's presence was frightening citizens and depressing real estate values. When Giblin asked him to describe the source of this information, Fisher replied that he had obtained it strictly from newspaper accounts, police reports, and explanations from Chicago crime investigators. He went on to say that associates of Capone were acknowledged notable gangsters such as Jack "Machine Gun" McGurn, and "Crane Neck" Nugent. But again, he confessed, this information had come from outside sources; he had no firsthand knowledge.

The prominent Miami Beach pioneer acknowledged that he had never been in Capone's house nor had he ever set eyes on Chicago's chief mobster until that day in court. When asked if he had given the order to station two Miami Beach cops outside Capone's home, he denied it. He did admit, however, that he had "suggested" the idea to city officials.

Giblin asked Fisher about his connection to gambling houses either in Miami or Montank Point, New York, where the businessman had other investments. He also asked about possible interest in the boat *Amphitrite*. Fisher denied both.[173] Had Giblin known about Fisher's yachts, which were "built with special between-deck compartments for shipments of Bimini Booze,"[174] he might have been able to further embarrass the respected businessman. It wasn't until June 10 that Judge Barns finally heard other witnesses in the case.

Over the course of several days in which the padlock case was heard, Capone appeared impeccably dressed for each occasion, bolstering his reputation as the country's best dressed hoodlum. One morning he appeared in a "gray suit, handkerchief and shirt to match, a dark blue tie with tiny white polka dots and sport shoes." On other days, his ensembles, which drew comments from many in the courtroom, were colorful outfits of white, tan, blue, and green.[175] Despite his snorky attire, however, Capone was about to hear witnesses whose testimony had the potential of exchanging his colorful hand-made garments for those with horizontal gray and white stripes.

Capone appeared in court impeccably dressed in custom-made suits that drew comments from many in the courtroom.

Witnesses Testify

Several men delivered what could have been damaging testimony. The first, Edward Robinson, a five-year resident of Palm Island, stated that the continual patrol by Miami Beach police at Capone's residence gave the appearance that the island was an "armed camp." He also swore that Capone's gangsters walked around the grounds of the Palm Island estate brandishing pistols on their hips. He stated further that every time a tire exploded on the causeway, he received a phone call asking if "warfare" had broken out on the island.[176] Under cross examination, Giblin tried to persuade Robinson to admit that he merely "thought" the objects were guns, but Robinson would not budge from his testimony.

The Reverend William H. Sledge of the West Little River Baptist Church told the court that while soliciting Capone to rent a car from him, he had witnessed one of the mobster's underlings giving a bootlegger an order to deliver a case of champagne and two cases of Scotch to the home of Fred Pine, candidate for county solicitor. Sledge couldn't identify Capone's brother John as the hoodlum and instead insisted that the man looked more like J. Fritz Gordon, one of Capone's attorneys.

Major George E. Brown, head of Army Corps of Engineers, testified that he had been called to the Capone home to investigate a complaint that Capone had "exceeded his authority" in constructing his dock. Brown said he found this to be true and ordered work to cease, pending application and approval of an additional permit. After Capone complied, he gave the Major a tour of his home and "attempted to press a banknote on him as a tip," but Brown refused. He did, however, accept a cigar.

As deliberations dragged on, it soon became obvious that some residents didn't think Capone was the negative influence he was made out to be. After all, many admitted to having accepted invitations to dine and drink at the gangster's estate.

The judge had to bring the courtroom under control several times with raps from his gavel when spectators broke into laughter as testimony turned almost comedic. It started as Wen R. Phillips, editor of *Miami Life*, asserted that "he had been a publisher since birth." Further testimony about his presence at the Capone home brought out the man's daily affinity for liquor, and when asked if he was drunk on the stand, Phillips refused to answer. He did admit, however, that while he hadn't had a drink that day, he had imbibed numerous drinks the day before.

Frank Gallant, an artisan, told of being employed by Capone for several months the previous summer to construct an addition on the home. While there, he admitted to having been in the home on numerous occasions for dinners and conferences when "drinks" were served and, in fact, he had consumed several himself. Questioned about what kind of drink it was, he replied a "highball." But when asked to describe what was in the drink, he flat out couldn't remember, "I drank something, I don't know what it was."[177]

Other testimony discredited high profile witnesses when they admitted to being just as "crooked" as Capone. For instance, Thomas J. Pancoast, president of the Chamber of Commerce, told how Capone's presence was corrupting the reputation of the area. He became "mortified," however, when he had to admit under oath that there were indeed slot machines in the basement of his own hotel on Miami Beach.[178]

Roddey Burdine, head of Miami's largest department store, had an embarrassing tale of his own. Testifying for the prosecution, the respected businessman was asked to define the term "gangster." He answered, "a man who kills when necessary; who carries his point with whatever weapon is at hand; who takes the law into his own hands . . . has no respect for law of decent society . . . makes his own laws . . . thinks nothing of human life or its sanctity." [179]

Later under cross examination, he confessed that the "gangster" Capone had made purchases at his store of "at least five figures."[180] Burdine's face turned a darker shade of pink when he was asked if he had ever visited the Capone residence to seek a donation to the local Community Chest[181] of which he was director. In response, he admitted that he had been there "only once" but hadn't seen Capone since. When asked about having been served liquor during that visit, Burdine initially refused to answer, stating that since he was a guest he thought it "against the etiquette of society" to do so. Judge Barns, however, ordered him to respond.

While Burdine replied that the question made him feel like "a stool pigeon,"[182] he nevertheless testified that on his visit Capone had invited him in to have a seat, some champagne, and a chat. Two hours later, Burdine said he walked away with a $1,000 donation and the strong suggestion that he arrange an introductory party for the Chicago gangland czar and his friends at a local country club. When members of the Community Chest discovered the deceptive gift, however, the party fell through and they returned the money.[183]

After dozens of witnesses had testified for the prosecution, the state rested its case. It was now time for Giblin and Gordon to put on their defense. Instead of calling even one witness, however, Capone's attorneys moved for an immediate dismissal. Their contention was that the state had not met their burden of proof.

Judge Barns deferred his decision until the next day.

Parties Successfully Mitigate Public Sentiment

Throughout Capone's arrests and litigation issues, he tried to win over public sentiment by throwing parties to which he invited the city's notables. Afternoon "teas" were held at his house in which poker became the centerpiece. Jack Sewell, of Sewell Brother's Store, attended one of the teas and years later recalled that the game was played with "nothing but $1,000 bills." He also noted that just after his arrival, Capone had lamented his loss by declaring, "I'm out, these scoundrels have taken me for $250,000!" Sewell also remarked that Jack "Greasy Thumb" Guzik was in attendance whom Capone introduced as the "father of the syndicate." He remembered the incident because it was the first time he had ever heard the term "syndicate."[184]

It wasn't just the adults Capone hoped to impress. Rumors of his enormous pool seemed to capture the imagination of many, including the students at St. Patrick. When one of Sonny's teachers mentioned that classmates would love to attend a swimming party hosted by the Capones, it sounded like the perfect opportunity for Palm Island's newest resident to demonstrate his hospitality, especially to Sonny's classmates.

On the day of the event, almost 75 children showed up at the party that was accessorized by balloons and noisemakers. They enjoyed swimming, lunch—chicken, cake, and soda—and games. Upon departure, each child was given a box of candy.[185]

In late May, Capone sent out fifty invitations for a dinner party and musicale. The *Miami Daily News* branded the soiree Capone's "coming out party" and "social debut." While 18 of the engraved invitations were reserved for his friends, 32 were sent through an agent to a select list of "approachable" Miamians. One went to a city official who refused the invite. Another was presented but later withdrawn when it was learned that the recipient was an employee of the *Miami Daily News*.[186]

Upon entering the Capone home, guests traded in their engraved invitations for an American flag pin. They were encouraged to remove their jackets and ties and to make themselves at home. Dinner consisted of spaghetti, steak, and ginger ale; the night was devoid of liquor. Among Capone's guests were attorneys, Giblin and Gordon, weekly newspaper publisher J.F. Wendler, two unnamed representatives of Miami funeral homes, and more than fifty others. The *Miami Daily News* noted that none of the guests were "recognized as 'leading business and professional men' for whom the dinner was reported to have been arranged."[187] Nevertheless, Capone's guests enjoyed the party, lauding him as a "new businessman in the community" and gifting him with a fountain pen.[188]

Some believed that in light of Capone's current court cases, the parties were held deliberately to sway public opinion. Mike Glenn, manager for Miami Beach developer Carl Fisher, wrote in a report to his boss: "In my opinion, he is trying to build up his case by attempting to show that reputable citizens here do not consider him undesirable."[189]

Padlock Case Concludes

On June 14, 1930, Judge Barns ruled in Capone's favor. Not doubting testimony that Capone had possessed liquor on his Palm Island property nor that residents didn't approve of him living on the island, the judge noted: "If a community is embarrassed by the mere presence of any particular individual, it certainly does not have to deal with him either socially or in business . . ." but if " . . . the only cause of annoyance is the mere presence of Al Capone upon the premises . . . the law does not provide for the expulsion of undesirables, as such."[190]

More Charges . . . This Time Perjury!

Capone was out of court a mere two hours when County Solicitor George E. McCaskill, who, at the time, was in a runoff election with former County Solicitor Fred Pine, hastily filed four perjury charges against Capone stemming from the false imprisonment hearing. At the time Giblin and Gordon were notified of the charges against their client, Capone had already boarded a boat for an outing on the bay. When he returned, Giblin accompanied him to court where the charges, to be tried separately, claimed Capone had lied during his false-imprisonment hearing. If convicted, Capone would face a possible 80 years in prison.

The charges were prepared by Richard H. Hunt, former assistant state attorney, who, just weeks prior, had been employed by McCreary and a group of other businessmen as special prosecutor.[191] McCaskill believed that if he won the case before the June 24th election, the conviction would give voters the impetus to cast their votes for him thereby allowing him to retain his post in a win over Pine.[192]

The charges claimed that Capone falsely testified regarding the following statements: that upon his arrest, McCreary had ordered his "personal items thrown into the toilet;" that McCreary had told him he would arrest him every time he set foot on the street even if his wife and son were with him; that he was not allowed to use the telephone to contact anyone, including his attorneys or family; and that McCreary had told prison attendants to hold Capone without food, water, or blankets. He was freed on a whopping $14,000 bond.[193]

Three weeks later, Warren L. Newcomb, peace justice, reopened Capone's case in order to allow Capone on the stand to "correct" testimony he had given during the initial hearing. Hunt, who protested this ruling, pointed out that if "any errors had been made by Capone he should have corrected them voluntarily, but that he waited until the criminal prosecution was started against him before he saw fit to attempt it." But Giblin argued that they had just discovered errors in the transcript and his client had the right to correct them. Incidentally, the Sunday prior to the hearing, Hunt's office had been broken into and the papers dealing with Capone's testimony had been scattered around the room.[194]

During the hearing, Giblin led Capone through a step-by-step reconsideration of his prior testimony in which he essentially recanted his assertions against McCreary. "I was excited . . . I wouldn't swear to it," Capone told the court.[195]

The cases were scheduled for trial in July, but Capone asked for a delay so he could take care of "urgent" business in Chicago. The request was denied. With the valuables charge already thrown out, on July 12 the second case concerning Capone's telephone charge came to trial. After Judge E.C. Collins rendered a verdict of not guilty on the telephone charge, McCaskill dropped the other perjury charges having been denied satisfaction on the first two.[196]

Capone Drawn into Campaign Battle without Consent

At the conclusion of the perjury cases, a brouhaha took place between incumbent County Solicitor George E. McCaskill and Fred Pine, former solicitor and McCaskill's current opponent. It all happened when

Capone was brought front and center into their political fight with the *Miami Daily News* rumor that Pine was friendly with Capone. Along with testimony that Pine had been supplied liquor by Capone, his "friendly" relationship with the mob boss could easily unhinge his political aspirations. In a signed statement that appeared on the front page of the June 17 *Miami Herald* (the paper that backed the former solicitor), Pine denied the rumor and challenged the *Miami Daily News* to submit proof of his relationship with Capone. That "proof" came in the form of a telegram.

T.W. "Tub" Palmer, former operator and owner of the Columbus hotel, wired the *Miami Daily News* from Atlanta where he was on business telling the paper that Pine had asked him to go over and meet Capone to prove that he was "a good fellow." After introductions, the three had remained at the home for two or three hours during which Pine and Capone had addressed each other "intimately as Fred and Al."

Pine sheepishly tried to extricate himself from the embarrassing situation by sending a letter to the editorial section of the *Miami Herald* in which he stated that it was true he had visited Capone sometime during the winter of 1928—1929. Pine went on to explain that while neither he nor Palmer was acquainted with Capone, he had gone to the home on Palmer's request and as his attorney because Palmer needed money and he wanted to see if Capone would lend it to him. Capone had refused.

Tub Palmer countered with a second telegram branding Pine's statement "a deliberate lie." He also wrote that Pine had never represented him in any legal matters, and that his statement was simply a "smoke screen to cover his visit and friendship with Capone."

On June 20, a political forum was held at a park in Little River with about 400 citizens in attendance. At the event, Pine turned the controversy into a campaign opportunity. "'I have never been a saint or a sinner,' he said in a final appeal to the pity of the crowd. 'I am just an average man caring for an aged mother, and I want you, those of you who believe in fair play, justice, democracy and the fundamental principles of democratic government to vote for me.'"[197]

Despite controversy throughout his campaign, Pine won the election.[198]

Seeking Respite from Litigation and Controversy

Exhausted from fighting communities and litigation in both Chicago and Miami, Capone yearned for the day when it would all be over and he could finally enjoy some long overdue South Florida peace and quiet. After all, that was the reason he said he had come to southern Florida in the first place. To make his vision a reality, he started looking for property outside the Miami area.

CHAPTER 9

CAPONE ISLAND

*It's hard, dangerous work, aside from any hate at all, and when a
fellow works hard at any line of business he wants to go
home and forget about it. He don't want to be afraid to sit near a
window or an open door.*[199]

Al Capone

In June of 1930, word was out that Giblin, on behalf of Capone, was looking for property out of the public eye both in northern Broward County and around Lake Okeechobee in Palm Beach County. The *Everglades News*, a publication of the town of Canal Point on the east bank of Lake Okeechobee, attributed this knowledge to W.G. "Guy" Stovall, a well-known contractor in Pahokee, Florida. Stovall, who claimed he had presented an offer to Capone for a block of land fronting the lake, said that Capone and others wanted the land for a hunting and fishing preserve.[200] While it is unknown whether this transaction was ever consummated, another well documented transaction took place in Deerfield.

Giblin, whose name is identified only as "trustee" on the June 30, 1930, deed, purchased a 50.2-acre tract of land in northern Broward County that abuts Palm Beach County. The land, a half mile from the closest road, was inaccessible by car.[201] Two days later "Capone Seeks Foothold in Broward" splashed across the headline of the *Fort Lauderdale*

Daily News in large bold type. The article announced: "What is believed to be a move on the part of Al Capone, Chicago beer and brothel baron, to establish residence and headquarters in Broward county was seen today with the filing of a deed at the Broward courthouse for transfer of a large tract of land lying between the Florida East Coast and Hillsborough canals at Deerfield . . ." When Giblin was asked about whether he had bought the property for his client, he smugly replied, "When I found out, I'll let you know."[202]

Confirmation of the land transfer to Vincent C. Giblin, trustee, was given by E.B. Davis, previous title holder, a day later in the *Palm Beach Post*. The article clearly associated Giblin, described as a former Broward judge and Capone's chief legal counsel, with the gangster, who they called a "notorious Chicago racketeer."[203] The inference on who had actually purchased the land was unmistakable.

Capone's purchase of land in Broward County was music to the ears of Dade County officials. As well, hopes ran high among Miami Beach citizens bent on ousting the gangster from their community that he would indeed take up residency in the county just north of Miami.[204]

About this time, W.D. McDougald, Deerfield Police Chief and a Sheriff's deputy, received a call from Broward County Sheriff Paul C. Bryan. Margaret McDougald Shadoin, a long time Deerfield Beach resident and daughter of the chief, recalled:

> *My dad was told Capone had purchased land on the peninsula, sight unseen, and was coming up to look at it. He wanted my dad and Deputy Alvin Stewart to escort the mobster and offer him protection because Capone was the target for an assassination at all times. Dad said Capone was a very mannerly person who told him he was planning to build a nightclub and casino on the island.*[205]

As soon as word got out about the land deal, speculation ran rampant as for what the property would be used. An article in the *Palm Beach Post* on July 15 confirmed some of that conjecture when it reported that work on clearing the land would begin immediately. Capone's new Florida residence, at a cost more than $375,000, would be built on the triangular-shaped land mass. Architectural plans and house construction would take up $250,000 of that figure. The remaining $125,000 in construction fees would include a 75- by 125-foot swimming pool. The information was reported to have come from W.G. Stovall of the firm Vivian and Stovall, a Lake Worth contractor.[206]

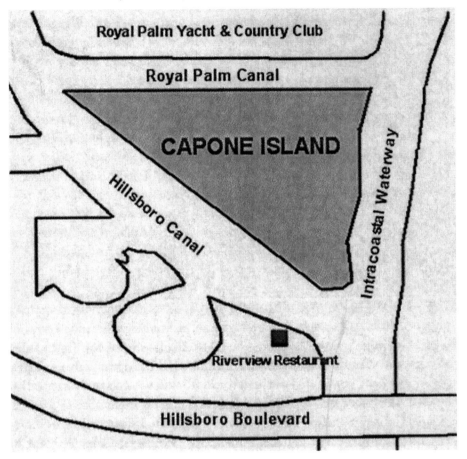

Vincent Giblin purchased this triangular plot of land in Deerfield, Florida, for his client Al Capone who, it was reported, hoped to build a home on it.

It is unclear why construction on the property didn't take place. Some accounts place the blame on inaccessibility of the land and that Boca Raton's town council may have thwarted efforts to facilitate that access. Broward County attorney William G. Crawford, who wrote several articles about Capone Island and Giblin, disputes this, however, with substantial documentation that access to the land had already been approved. Given Capone's on-going legal battles and the fact that in October 1931 he was sentenced to ten years in federal prison for income tax evasion, Crawford concluded that it made sense that it was for financial reasons, and not legal ones, that construction was abandoned. With Capone in prison, "Giblin would have no reason to retain title of the property for Capone's benefit," he noted.

Unpaid taxes began to accumulate on the property, and in 1934, Giblin quitclaimed the deed back to Davis. By this time, at least five years of back taxes were owed the City of Deerfield. The land was subsequently purchased by Florida Inland Navigational District (FIND) from the town of Deerfield at a tax foreclosure sale. They, in turn, conveyed the property to the state on a ninety-nine-year-right to use it as a park and recreation area.[207] It is now a Broward County park called Deerfield Island and is accessible only by launch from Sullivan Park across the canal from the park close to where the Riverview restaurant once stood.

As a side note, when growing up in Deerfield Beach David Eller heard rumors that Capone had hidden a lot of money on the island. As a teen, he spent many hours with friends swimming over to the island to dig holes and look for Capone's hidden treasure. He said of his efforts: "The only things we actually got were blisters and sandspurs."[208]

Yet digging for Al Capone's buried treasure isn't so farfetched. Before he went to jail in 1932, he had stashed almost $100 million dollars under assumed names in safety deposit boxes in different banks in the U.S. and Cuba. Keys to each box were tagged and the name used on the account written on the tag. All the keys were then placed in a strong box and buried.

After Capone's release from prison in 1939, he went back to the place where he thought he had buried the box. He couldn't find it. He continued searching, but the strong box never materialized. Capone's brother Ralph commandeered several friends to help him dig up the yards at Al's homes on Prairie Avenue and Palm Island. Still nothing. In desperation, Ralph had Al hypnotized. That, too, was to no avail.[209]

The box containing Capone's keys still remains buried out there somewhere.

CHAPTER 10

THE END IS NEAR

It's pretty tough when a citizen with an unblemished record must be hounded from his home by the very policemen whose salaries are paid, at least in part, from the victim's pocket.[210]

Al Capone

"C issy" Medill Patterson, who ran the Washington *Herald* for newspaper publishing mogul William Randolph Hearst, was in Miami in early January 1931 when, on a whim, she decided to drive up to Capone's estate on Palm Island. Brandishing the same affinity he had shown for all media personalities, Capone invited the journalist in, offered to show her around, and treated her to a refreshing glass of lemonade. Patterson described Capone:

> *He has the neck and shoulders of a wrestler. One of those prodigious Italians, thick-chested, close to six feet tall. The muscles of his arms stretched the sleeves of his light brown suit, so that it seemed to be cut too small for him.*

> *Once I looked at his eyes. Ice-gray, ice-cold eyes. You can't anymore look into the eyes of Capone than you can look into the eyes of a tiger . . .*

Patterson stayed to question Capone at length. One of her questions dealt with the subject of Prohibition—Did he think it would be repealed?

"Yes, I do, and I'm all for that time to come. Prohibition has made nothing but trouble—trouble for all of us. Worst thing ever hit the country," he told her.[211]

It was one of his only statements with which a majority of U.S. citizens agreed.

Miami Beach Clamps Lid on Crime

Miami Beach had long been a cesspool of corruption, but with Capone's presence the stink had bubbled to the surface causing leading citizens to shout "Enough!" The Committee of 100, business and civic leaders who had banded together to improve and promote the community, had been around for a few years, but instead of growth and improvement, they had seen their city deteriorate. On January 14, 1931, a gathering of almost one hundred of the city's biggest taxpayers and most widely known citizens took place in Miami Beach council chambers to register a "ringing protest against license for outlawry."

Leading the outcry was John B. "Jack" Orr Sr., Miami's celebrated builder, business leader philanthropist, civic supporter, member of the Committee of 100, and one of Greater Miami's most beloved citizens. As a Palm Island resident, he was aligned with the Palm & Hibiscus Islands Improvement Association, Inc. and was a staunch and outspoken proponent of removing not only Capone from Palm Island but eradicating gambling and corruption from Miami Beach, blights that seemed to have permeated the very fabric of the community. Others in attendance included: Carl G. Fisher, Joseph H. Adams. N.B.T. Roney, Clayton Sedgwick Cooper, T.J. and Arthur Pancoast, Dan Hardie, Judge J. Julian Sutherland, Irving A. Collins, C. W. Chase, and dozens of other prominent citizens.

Orr was the first and principal speaker. His impassioned plea took place over the objection of his physician as Orr had been weakened by a long illness and several operations that left him quite frail. He was so concerned that Miami Beach was failing prey to racketeers and gamblers, that he mustered the strength to denounce the dire situation: "Miami beach has prostituted its civic soul and has raised an illegitimate progeny of low-brow people who have become a menace to the community."

One after another, those in attendance spoke before the assembly in which "strong men used strong language and banged their points home with hard fists." The speakers described how present lifestyles and future businesses were being threatened by the rampant illegal activities on the Beach and called for the city to return to a "God-fearing, law abiding community" or it would slip into the hands of racketeers. Capone's name came up several times in that his presence was accused of "undermining the moral fiber of the community."[212] But their concerns weren't just about Capone. City officials, law enforcement agencies, and prominent citizens had also contributed to the problem by insisting on a "liberal policy."[213] Now, it was time to reign in the illegal activities, even if it meant cleaning house in the police department.

Mayor Val Cleary said that as far as he knew the Beach was closed to illegal activity and that the chief of police had his orders. If the chief didn't do his job, however, the mayor wouldn't hesitate to remove him. To the cheers of those in attendance, Councilman Meade promised that the racketeers would be cleaned out.[214]

Orr hoped his appeal would result in a better life for those who lived in Miami Beach and never thought for a moment he would become the brunt of a brutal attack because of his conviction.

Orr Assaulted by Capone's Henchmen

Carol Orr Hartman, granddaughter of John B. Orr Sr. wrote: "When Capone found out that my grandfather [John B. Orr Sr.] owned a home down the street from him, he became furious, so he had his henchman beat up my grandfather on one of his nightly walks around the island, putting him in the hospital."[215]

No "official" record of the assault was found, and, in fact, the assault wasn't publicly known until after Orr's death. It was, however, remembered quite vividly by John Orr Jr. who was 13 at the time of the beating. He went on to practice law, serve two terms in the Florida Legislature, and become Mayor of Dade County.

The *Miami Daily News* mentioned the incident when they wrote a tribute to Jack Orr Jr. after his death in 1974:

Jack Orr's father was a crime-fighting Dade Grand Jury foreman during the time when mobster Al Capone lived near him on Palm Island. There was an ambush one night, and a brutal beating, and a few months later the victim, Jack Orr's father, died of his injuries . . . He [Jack Orr Jr.] never lost in the years to follow his deep hatred for organized crime and the political corruption which tolerates it.[216]

Dade County's Civic Digest described the attack as follows:

"Forced to fight barehanded against armed men for his very life, a sickly citizen of peaceful pursuits against several thugs, he may be called a martyr because that undoubtedly caused his relapse . . . Yet to be told is the full story of his being attacked by Capone-inspired thugs almost in front of his own home on Palm Island. They had to attack him there because he refused to be cowed by superior force when they demanded that he go for a ride . . . Mr. Orr fought with his fists against their guns and blackjacks. They downed him but were frightened off . . .[217]

John. B. Orr Sr., prominent builder, resident of Palm Island, and staunch opponent of Capone's presence in Miami Beach, was assaulted by Capone's henchmen. *Photo courtesy of Carol Orr Hartman.*

Obviously, Capone didn't realize the builder was so beloved by Floridians. When John Orr Sr. returned from medical treatment at the Mayo Clinic two years prior to the attack, he received "one of the most spontaneous and genuine mass tributes ever paid a citizen of Miami or Florida. At almost every stop in his train ride from Jacksonville southward, Mr. Orr was cheered to the echo [by Shriners]. His welcome was of the nature usually accorded only a president of the United States."[218]

Upon Jack Orr Sr.'s death from his illness and injuries on August 28, 1932, the *Miami Daily News* ran a two-page spread on his background, including glowing tributes by many of the city's top business, civic, and political leaders.[219]

Old Ledgers Prove Key to Government's Case

Over a period of several years, the government had knitted together a team of U.S. treasury agents headed by the savvy Elliot Ness. The group was called "The Untouchables," indicative of their reputations as straight arrows and their inability to be bought off. Their job was to curb mob activity with their primary goal to get Capone. The group's concerted efforts disrupted Capone's businesses and snatched a number of his Outfit off the street, but Capone was not among them. What they needed was solid evidence of income so they could arrest him for failure to pay taxes. But Internal Revenue agents were finding this a difficult task as relayed in this letter from W.C. Hodkins, Jaque L. Westrich, and H.N. Clagett:

> *Capone never had a bank account and only on occasion could it be found where he ever endorsed a check, all of his financial transactions being made in currency. Agents were unable to find where he had ever purchased any securities, therefore, any evidence secured had to be developed through the testimony of associates or others, which, through fear of personal injury, or loyalty, was most difficult to obtain.[220]*

Since they couldn't find any property, bank accounts, or stocks listed in his name, evidence was in short supply. Frank Wilson, an investigative accountant, would prove to be the linchpin in the discovery of that evidence.

One night after everyone else had retired for the evening, Wilson decided to do a once over on the records he had already examined; perhaps he had missed something. About 1 a.m. the next morning weary from his tedious work, he went to return the documents to the filing cabinet. As he did so, he accidently bumped the drawer, slamming it shut. When he couldn't find the key, he went into an adjoining room where he located an old unlocked filing cabinet.

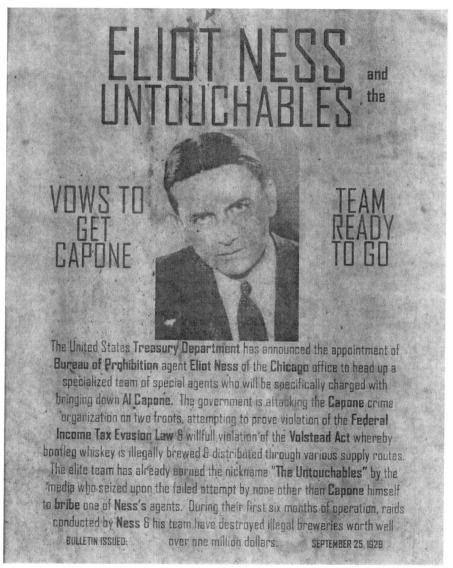

Eliot Ness of the United States Treasury Department vowed to "Get Capone!"

To make room for his files, he removed numerous dust encrusted envelopes from the drawer. Behind them was "a heavy package covered in brown paper." After cutting the binding, Wilson discovered three Capone ledgers. Entries in the second ledger—years 1924 to 1926—indicated revenues in the amount of $587,721.95 from a "large-scale gambling operation." Subsequent pages indicated payouts to a number of men in Capone's Outfit. But the nail in Capone's coffin was the entry at the top of one of the pages: "Frank Paid 17500 for Al." After subtracting all the payouts from the revenues, this amount matched the house profits. It was the evidence they had spent years looking for. Now all Frank needed was someone who could tie Capone to the ledger.

Three people had written in the ledgers, but only one person's handwriting was "neat and precise." Problem was they didn't know to whom it belonged. At a Cicero bank, the feds found a signature on a deposit slip that proved to be an undisputable handwriting match.

Following a tip, Wilson located Leslie Adelbert Shumway in Miami at the Biscayne Bay Kennel Club where he was working as a cashier. Though he feigned ignorance, "Oh, you're mistaken, Mr. Wilson, I don't know Al Capone," Wilson sent Shumway a decided message— "Play ball, Lew, and I'll guarantee that Mrs. Shumway will not become a widow."[221]

It was brought out in the trial that Capone had lived in luxury from the profits of his rackets. Tales of elaborate purchases—$12,500 automobiles, $135 suits, $30 shirts—were detailed to the jury. Countering the prosecution, Capone's attorneys brought in witnesses who testified of the mob kingpin's losses—$327,000 on horse racing bets alone in a five-year period. In the end, the amount of income tax the government claimed Capone owed was $215,000. Penalties, fines and taxation on other income, were expected to double that figure.[222]

On the twenty-three counts in the federal indictment, Capone was found not guilty on 18 of the charges. He was found guilty on five other charges—three on tax evasion and two on failure to file tax returns. The three counts of tax evasion, felonies, carried a possible five-year sentence and $10,000 fine each; the two misdemeanor charges each carried a possible one year prison term and a $10,000 fine.[223] Liens in the amount of $40,000, on which Mae was also named, were attached to the Palm Island home.[224]

The day before sentencing was to take place, Mike Ahern, Capone's attorney, appeared in court minus Capone and asked for a continuance. Capone, who was in Miami at the time, was tied up in civil litigation. On condition that Capone would immediately begin his jail term once sentence was pronounced, the judge agreed to postpone sentencing until July 30, 1931.[225]

Giblin and Capone Pull a Fast One?

Capone owed Giblin and Gordon $50,000 for their legal services. When several forceful reminders of payment due went unanswered, Giblin went to his client's Palm Island home to request payment. Upon arrival, Capone stopped him on the welcome mat pistol in hand. Outraged, Giblin countered, "You #&*! I dare you to shoot! You don't have the guts to shoot!" Reluctant to face a murder charge without a local lawyer by his side, Capone backed down. Giblin left without payment and filed suit in Dade County Circuit Court asking that Capone's furnishings be seized to satisfy the unpaid legal debt.

Riding lead in a convoy of moving vans on June 6, 1931, Giblin and Dade County deputy sheriffs entered Capone's Palm Island estate and began hauling away wicker sun porch furniture, beds and sofas. After a "clamorous discussion on the lawn," between Giblin and Capone, the gang lord agreed to pay.[226]

Whether the suit was devised to delay Capone's return to federal court in Chicago for sentencing or whether it was legit is unclear; however, Capone settled Giblin's suit for $10,000. Out of these proceeds, the attorney agreed to pay a "$1,000 bond and to represent all members of the [Capone] household, at no further charge, in matters pending."[227]

The suit was a lackluster ending to Giblin's and Gordon's relationship with Capone who, for four months, had competently defended the Chicago gangster against every civil and criminal case Miami and Dade County authorities had thrown at him. Giblin later said of his time as the gangland leader's attorney: "The last thing in the world I wanted right then was a criminal practice but suddenly I had it and it cost me money. Some of my best business clients dropped me like a hot potato. It was not politically expedient to have been Capone's attorney."[228]

Sentencing Announced

Capone returned to Chicago for sentencing and had hoped to serve his felony sentences concurrently, but the judge thought otherwise. He was sentenced to serve two of the five-year felony sentences consecutively—a total of ten years in a federal prison—with an additional one year term in county jail for the misdemeanor. Fines totaled $50,000 with $7,692.29 tacked on in court costs.[229]

Al Capone's criminal record. *Photo courtesy of Federal Bureau of Investigation*

Upon hearing the sentence the "200-pound gang chief made no attempt to conceal his rage," and when an internal revenue agent, who was considerably smaller than Capone, approached him to present liens attaching his Palm Island property for overdue income taxes, the now convicted felon started for the man as if to hit him. At the county jail where he was subsequently taken, he also attempted to strike a photographer with a water bucket, shouting, "I'll knock your block off!" Guards hustled him back to a cell.[230]

Incarceration

Capone was held in Chicago's Cook County jail without bond pending appeals. Because the judge refused to allow him to serve his year's misdemeanor sentence first, he would also remain in the facility until his felony sentence started in federal prison without any reduction for time served.

Al Capone was incarcerated at Alcatraz, known as "The Rock," where he spent seven years serving two consecutive prison sentences for income tax evasion. *Photo courtesy of Richard Hall.*

On May 3, 1932, Capone was transferred by train to the federal penitentiary at Atlanta, Georgia, where he became prisoner number 40886. Two years later, he was whisked away by rail, along with 52 other prisoners from the Atlanta penitentiary, to a faraway California island where an old military prison had been refurbished into the fed's newest inescapable maximum security prison—Alcatraz.

He became prisoner number 85 and lived in cell 181, a 5- by 9-foot room that had a dropdown bunk, toilet, washstand, table, and chair. Only two immediate family members were allowed to visit him in a month, no exceptions. It was the first time Capone's influence over prison officials and guards remained in check. As with his incarceration in Pennsylvania, he became a model prisoner.[231] On the outside, the government was still out to satisfy liens against his properties in order to pay off his income tax debt.

In Alcatraz, Al Capone became prisoner number 85. *Photo courtesy of Federal Bureau of Investigation..*

Tax Liens Accumulate Against Capone Properties

"Court costs, attorney fees and large income tax liens have used up all of Capone's ready cash and forced him to put heavy encumbrances against the only real property he owns," reported the *Palm Beach Daily News* in 1938.[232] Aside from the $40,000 a year it cost to maintain his household at Palm Avenue, which seemed to miraculously appear ("the outfit took care of him"),[233] he was desperate to raise the necessary capital to pay off his federal debt. In 1936 from behind Alcatraz bars, he had signed over power of attorney to a D.C. lawyer to raise $100,000. These funds, however, were insufficient as liens continued to accumulate. Things became so critical that at one time Capone even deliberated about doing something he loathed to consider—hire a ghost writer to pen his biography.[234] In the end, monies raised and those that came from the Outfit (Frank Nitti became the Outfit's new boss after Capone went to prison) proved sufficient. Capone never wrote his life's account and Mae never lost her Palm Island home.

Capone occupied a 5- by 9-foot cell while in Alcatraz. *Photo courtesy of Richard Hall.*

Dalliances Return to Haunt Capone

While incarcerated in Atlanta, Capone had been given a Wasserman test to detect syphilis. The results proved positive at level 2[235] (the scale goes from 1 to 4 indicating the severity of the condition).[236] Urologist Dr. Steven T. Brown treated him with injections of heavy metals and arsenicals, the only treatment available prior to the development of penicillin.

By 1938, Alcatraz's most infamous prisoner was displaying disturbing signs—confusion, combative and compulsive behavior, shuffling gait, and wandering consciousness. Syphilis was suspected as the catalyst of Capone's confusing behavior and this was confirmed with a spinal tap that resulted in a positive Wasserman of 4 plus. Capone spent the rest of his sentence in the prison hospital under treatment. This would not become public knowledge until after his death.[237]

Capone's stay in Alcatraz came to an end on January 6, 1939. He was subsequently transferred to Terminal Island, a Federal Correctional Institution in California, where, under a doctor's care, he served his one-year misdemeanor sentence.[238] To Capone's family, this "cure" was more deadly than the disease and had immediate effects on all of Capone's bodily functions.[239]

In mid-November, he was finally released.[240] His discharge to family and doctors in Gettysburg, Pennsylvania, came with "the drama and secrecy of a spy swap—at a designated crossroads twelve miles east of town." He was admitted to Union Memorial hospital under the care of Dr. Moore and remained there until March 19, 1940, when treatment ended.[241]

Capone returned to Miami Beach just 30 hours later.

CHAPTER 11

Capone's Final Days

All I ever did was sell beer and whiskey to our best people.
All I ever did was supply a demand that was pretty
popular. Why, the very guys that made my trade good are
the ones that yell the loudest about me. Some of the leading
judges use the stuff.[242]

Al Capone

Capone's days in Miami were filled with relaxation—fishing, boating, swimming, card games—and family. While the former mob kingpin was much improved, he was still far from his former self.

Documents obtained from the family of the late Dr. Kenneth Phillips of Miami, Capone's primary physician, included a letter from Dr. Joseph Moore, the Baltimore syphilis specialist that was involved with Capone's treatment. In his lengthy letter written in 1941, Moore suggested that the Capone family hire a male nurse who could pose as a chauffeur to "protect the public from the gangster's dementia-driven violent outbursts." Moore went on to say, "If, by any chance, Mr. Capone makes an unprovoked attack upon a stranger, he is very likely to find himself in court for disturbing the peace and, as a result of that, to be recognized insane by the judge and to be committed to a Florida psychiatric hospital."

Moore asserted that the treatment Capone had received had increased his mental and intelligence quotient from that of a 7-year-old to an age 14 range, but that he was still "silly, childish and mentally deteriorated."[243]

While penicillin had been recognized in 1891, it wasn't until 1939 that English researchers were able to demonstrate its ability to kill infectious bacteria. Mass production of the drug, however, was still years off, and with England fully entrenched in WWII, whatever amounts of the powerful drug that were being produced remained restricted to injured soldiers on the battle front.[244]

In 1942, Dr. Moore was finally able to obtain an adequate amount of the drug to treat Capone, the first patient with neurosyphilis to receive the miracle drug. While it extended Capone's remission from the disease's more incapacitating effects, treatment came too late to cure him.[245]

FBI Stakeout 93 Palm Avenue

In 1945, the Federal Bureau of Investigation (FBI) conducted a three-week stakeout of Capone's residence on Palm Island hoping to catch Matthew Capone, Al's brother, wanted on a charge of murder. During the 24-hour surveillance, agents fastidiously recorded the comings and goings at the house and their observations of guests visiting the estate.

Agents reported to J. Edgar Hoover that Capone was living a "quiet life." Many days he sat in his stripped pajamas by the pool or fished from his dock. His routine outside the residence consisted of visits to the grocery story, dentist, and drives to see Sonny, then living near Hollywood, Florida. Inside his home, Capone was reported to have occasional visits from his old friends from syndicate days in Chicago in which his speech was described as rapid and his words slurred. It was also noted that he constantly hummed, whistled, and sang.[246]

The once animated and mobile life of the Chicago Outfit's kingpin had been reduced to a reclusive tranquil one with few, if any, responsibilities or cares.

Capone Deteriorates

One day Miami Beach rookie cop Pat Purdue recognized Capone strolling along Lincoln Road in Miami Beach. Capone had always had nothing but respect for the boys in blue and addressed the officer in his usual friendly style, "How are you today, pal?" Purdue responded, "Fine," and didn't notice anything unusual until Capone repeated his greeting another three times. After a brief conversation when Purdue recalled the time he had caddied for the gang boss back in 1928, Capone offered the officer a stick of Dentyne gum. He apparently gave a piece to everyone he met.[247]

Al Capone spent many of his final days in his pajamas by his pool or fishing from his boat.

Capone's mental capacity had deteriorated so badly that the family had to devise two "trick" telephone numbers for him to call should he be out of the house and become separated from his bodyguards. These numbers were "drilled into him by the family." The numbers, which were neither listed in the telephone directory or information, consisted of two alternating digits, beginning with either one, that when dialed in a certain sequence, connected to the house. The only catch was that the correct key numbers had to come first and if that was missed, which happened occasionally, he would have to start the sequence over again.[248]

Neighbors described Capone as a "physical and mental wreck," with his only physical exercise being batting a tennis ball against a wall with a racket. While he attempted to play gin rummy, family and friends who played with him placated him by allowing him to win. A visitor who was not accustomed to this routine, however, beat Capone one day. He was reported to have flown into a rage and shouted, "Get the boys. I want them to take care of this wise guy."[249]

Chicago Christmas

In December of 1946, Capone returned to his Prairie Avenue home in Chicago, spending his last Christmas with his family. Deidra Capone, Al's niece, described him as wearing a "white shirt, cufflinks that sparkled, and a tie held in place with a stick pin in the form of a woman's face." The family was decked out in their Sunday best and sat at the dinner table with Al at the head.

The Christmas tree had the usual ornaments and candles but it was also decorated with United States savings bonds in the amount of one thousand dollars. Deidra wrote, "The money flowed when Al was around. He may have successfully hidden his assets from the federal government, but he never hid them from his family. The outfit had their own retirement plan, and they took care of Al and his wife and son as long as they lived."[250]

Capone's Last Birthday

Before the beginning of the New Year, Mae and Al returned to their Palm Island home in Miami Beach. With his 47th birthday right around the corner, Mae planned a homecoming birthday party to be attended by Miami's elite society. Al became quite ill not long after the party,[251] and the Capone family was summoned to Palm Island.

On January 21, 1947, Mae was awakened at 3:30 a.m. by "loud and sterterous type of breathing [a harsh snoring or gasping sound]" coming from her husband. When she administered water, he strangled. He then experienced several convulsions. Dr. Phillips examined him about 5:00 a.m. and found—"limbs spastic, face drawn, pupils dilated, and eyes abd [sic] jaws were set . . . left arm and leg were paralyzed." After treating Capone, Phillips noted that his blood pressure and heart rate returned to normal. He was administered oxygen through a mask and several male nurses were assigned to attend him.

By the next day, the paralysis was subsiding and Capone was almost back to normal. He did, however, complain of pain in both shoulders and there was a deep ulcer on his left foot which the doctor treated. The doctor also noted congestion in his chest. A number of drugs were administered, including penicillin.

On the 24th, Capone experienced bronchial spasms. Dr. Arthur Logie, a Miami lung specialist, was called in as a consultant and confirmed what Phillips surmised—Capone had both pneumonia and a failing heart.[252]

A house full of relatives and friends held vigil as Capone, "laid in bed, eyes closed, and continued his labored breathing." A priest called in by Mae offered prayers while Capone's mother wept, fingered her rosary, and offered supplications.[253]

Death Watch

With the first word that Capone was seriously ill, media gathered outside the front gate awaiting even a scrap of news regarding his deteriorating condition. "My grandfather [Ralph] asked them to leave us alone but they wouldn't, so he finally took some beer out to them. To my family, liquor solved everything," wrote Deidra Capone.[254]

Louie, one of Capone's crew, dutifully guarded the compound and opened the door only after inspecting and approving the caller through a slit in the front portal, a scene that conjured up former speakeasy days when his boss was king.[255] Dr. Phillips periodically fed the media his patient's latest condition. Headlines followed, except in the Miami Daily News. Cox proclaimed that Capone's death would be treated like any other obituary. "I don't want that son of a bitch on my front page," he said.[256]

At Hialeah race track and amongst the bookies and racketeers that gathered at 23rd Street near Collins Avenue, hushed talk turned to Capone. Some spoke with utter respect for the gang lord who had amassed such a vast empire in his years as head of the Outfit while others spoke of him with contempt for ending up a "chump."[257]

On the 25th, Capone rallied and felt well enough to swim laps in the pool. After that, he took a shower with the help of his nurses. As the men got ready to sprinkle talcum powder on his skin, he dropped to the floor, ". . . dead in an instant from a massive stroke," wrote Deidre Capone.[258]

One of his attendants called downstairs to Mae, who immediately came up to her husband's room. She gasped upon seeing his lifeless body. Rivulets of tears flowing down her cheeks spoke volumes. She dropped to her knees, whispered something to her beloved husband, and kissed his forehead.[259]

Capone's death certificate noted his death at 7:25 p.m. The cause was cited as "Bronchopneumonia - 48 hours, due to Apoplexy - 4 days."[260]

Al Capone's death certificate. *Image courtesy of National Archives and Records Administration.*

Family Chooses Privacy

News of Capone's death was withheld from the press for an hour due to Mae's collapse that necessitated medical attention. Since funeral arrangements remained secret, the only thing the press was told was that the details had not yet been finalized.[261] In reality, however, funeral arrangements had been made days before with Rago Brothers funeral homes in Chicago poised to transport Capone's body back to the city for burial.

To elude the press, Philbrick Funeral Home in Miami hustled Capone's body away in a regular car, after which, Lou Rago and his brother drove straight through to the Windy City.[262] In the meantime, Philbrick drove a hearse up to the Capone home. Not long after, the vehicle drove out of the estate with reporters following it. The funeral director said he had received instructions from Ralph that only family would attend the wake, scheduled for the next day, and the casket would be opened only when the family was present.[263]

The wake, with its closed and empty coffin, was attended by family and a "host of big shots from Florida, including Desi Arnaz Jr. . . ." Two days later, the family returned to Chicago by train, along with the empty coffin.[264]

Capone's remains first rested at the Mount Olivet cemetery in Chicago's far South Side between the graves of his father, Gabriele, and brother, Frank. In March of 1950, however, all three were moved to Mount Carmel Cemetery on the far West Side.[265]

Let Us Blush

The *Miami Daily News* which had followed Capone's every step, every arrest, every court case, ran an editorial the day after Capone died, and, it seemed, the paper would have the last word. The article lamented the fact that Capone had not died on the gallows, as he so richly deserved, but met his maker in his plush Palm Island estate, surrounded by luxury. Because of this, it was, the paper explained, a time for Miamians to:

> *. . . pause for a moment's meditation, a moment in the valley of humiliation where we belong . . . Only the national government halted him, and then only as a tax dodger, not as the murderous gangster which he was . . . His evil was stronger and braver than our good . . . We shall blush, and blush, and blush, resolved henceforth to be upstanding men, not pusillanimous crawlers before an underworld . . . Only*

because we were as we were, could Al Capone be as Al Capone was. Yes, let us blush.[266]

Mae Capone

In February of 1952, Mae sold her 93 Palm Avenue home to Thomas Warren Miller, a Cleveland real estate broker. The price was just over $64,000. That same year, she also sold her home on Prairie Avenue in Chicago.

Throughout Mae's marriage to Al, she remained loyal. "The public has one idea of my husband. I have another. I will treasure my memory and I always will love him," she said after Al died.[267]

Mae remained in Florida and lived an unassuming life until her death in 1986.[268]

CHAPTER 12

SINS OF THE FATHER

*I wanted to stop all that because I couldn't stand hearing my little kid
ask why I didn't stay home. I had been living at the Hawthorne Inn
for fourteen months . . . If it wasn't for him, I'd have said, "To hell
with you fellows. We'll shoot it out.*[269]

Al Capone

No doubt Albert Francis "Sonny" Capone had to deal with more family issues than most. After all, his first appearance, on December 4, 1918, in Brooklyn, New York, was to unwed mother, Mae Josephine Coughlin and rising gangster Alphonso "Al" Gabriele Capone. While the two married several weeks later, it was his father's nefarious activities and reputation that would dog Sonny the rest of his life.

Sonny's first challenge came at age seven when he was diagnosed with a bacterial infection of his mastoid, the bone behind his ear. Some accounts note he acquired this condition as the result of syphilis having been passed on to him. The condition is called congenital syphilis.[270] Sonny's condition became so severe that the family consulted specialists in New York. Radial surgery appeared the only viable solution (penicillin wasn't available to the general public until the 1940s). The procedure left

Sonny partially deaf and he had to wear a hearing aid. For a child with an infamous surname and having to wear a hearing device, it's no wonder he remained shy and a target for bullies. This led to his being enrolled in a number of different schools.[271]

Capone idolized his son often taking Sonny to baseball games, or spending time at home playing board games or listening to music on the gramophone. When he moved his family to Florida, he often took Sonny out on the bay in his boat.

Chicago Cubs catcher Gabby Hartnett talks with Sonny and Al Capone at a game at Wrigley Field in Chicago.

Sonny attended school at St. Patrick Catholic School, a private school in Miami Beach. It was there he met and became close friends with Desi Arnaz III, a young Cuban[272] whose parents had fled Cuba. The boys got together at 93 Palm Avenue every day after school to sing and play the bongos. Sonny also confided in Desi, a relationship Mae believed was "good for both of them" since they were only children with fathers that had been imprisoned.[273] (Desi Arnaz Sr. had been mayor of Santiago, Cuba, before serving in the Cuban House of Representatives. He was imprisoned during the Cuban revolution and fled to Florida after his release in 1933.)[274]

Carolyn Brimberry Orr, who lived on Palm Island just down the street from the Capones, attended St. Patrick Catholic School with Sonny. She told her daughter Carol Orr Hartman, that: "He was very antisocial and didn't interact with any of the kids. The mob kids that went to St. Pat's lived very secluded lives and weren't allowed to interact with the other children. They had bodyguards drop them off and pick them up at school."[275]

When Al was sent to Alcatraz, Sonny and Mae visited him. Deidra Capone described the visit as a "life-changing" experience for Sonny: "He was a teenager raised in luxury by a very protective and kind mother and educated in a private school built with his father's dollars. His father had once been king of Chicago and the social czar of Miami, and now Sonny had to see him reduced to a life unfit for any human being. Many years later, Sonny himself told me about his experience at Alcatraz with tears in his eyes."[276]

While Al was in Alcatraz, Sonny, 17, was arrested for reckless driving. Having ploughed into a stand of trees while trying to pass another vehicle at Washington Avenue and 15th Street in Miami Beach, he received minor injuries and was treated at St. Francis Hospital. He also had to post a $150 reckless driving bond.[277]

After high school, Sonny tried to extricate himself from the aura that surrounded the Capone name and attended Notre Dame University using the last name of Brown. When he was discovered to be Capone's son, however, he transferred to the University of Miami. He graduated with a B.S. degree in Business Administration then put his education to work in The Little Flower shop (1416 Washington Avenue, Miami Beach), owned by his uncle Dennis Coughlin, Mae's brother.

When war broke out, he left the flower shop to do his patriotic duty. Although he was exempt from military service because of his deafness, he went to work for the War Department at the Miami Air Depot as a mechanic's apprentice on an aircraft assembly line. After the war, he sold used cars but quit when he discovered the owner was rolling back the odometers.[278]

Sonny wed Diana Ruth "Boogie" Casey, his high school sweetheart and Miami University classmate, at St Patrick's Church in Miami Beach on December 30, 1941.[279] Three hundred guests attended the ceremony along with Al and Mae, one of their rare public appearances after his release from prison.[280] The couple had four daughters, Teresa, Veronica, Diane, and Barbara.[281]

For several years, Mae and Sonny ran an Italian restaurant at 6970 Collins Avenue with Diana Coughlin, Mae's sister-in-law. First called "Ted's Grotto," the restaurant was later renamed simply "The Grotto." [282] Mae served as cashier while Sonny worked as the maître d. The restaurant failed, however, and Sonny went to work for a tire company.

At a low ebb both emotionally and financially, Sonny was approached by his father's Outfit who offered to cut him in on some action. When he discussed it with his mother, Mae replied, "Your father broke my heart. Don't you break it."[283] While the opportunity may have brought him great wealth, Sonny remained straight.

For years, Mae and Sonny lived peaceful lives in relative obscurity, but that all changed when a new TV show hit the airwaves. Featuring Eliot Ness, a fictionalized version of a deceased prohibition agent of the same name who fought crime in Chicago in the 1930s, the pilot TV show began with a two-part series entitled "The Untouchables," later retitled "The Scarface Mob." Actor Neville Brand played Al Capone and the series ended with the mob boss's conviction and imprisonment.[284]

The show was produced by Sonny's old St. Patrick school chum Desi Arnaz III. He had moved to California, married Lucille Ball, and gone on to have an illustrious career on TV during the 1950s with the *I Love Lucy* show.[285] He later became a producer forming Desilu productions with his wife. (They went on to produce numerous TV shows in the 50s and 60s, among them "The Andy Griffith Show," "My Three Sons," "The Dick Van Dyke Show," and "Star Trek.")[286]

With the impending TV show, Mae and Sonny felt as though they had been stabbed to the bone. Sonny phoned Arnaz and asked him "for old time's sake to scrap the idea."[287] By that time, however, the show was already in production. Mae and Sonny filed a $6 million suit in 1959 against Desilu Productions, producer of "The Untouchables," and Allied Artists, producers of the movie "Al Capone," for failure to receive permission to use Capone's name or likeness. They claimed "The Untouchables" invaded their privacy and caused them "extreme humiliation." While they lost their suit in both the U.S. District and Circuit Courts in Chicago, they were hopeful the U.S. Supreme court would rule in their favor. It wasn't until 1965 that Mae and Sonny received the devastating news: the United States Supreme Court refused to hear their case.

While the high court didn't give a reason, the U.S. District and Circuit Courts in Chicago said: "Fictionalization and even distortion of a dead man's career does not invade the privacy of his relatives or friends." Attorneys for the defendants pointed out: "No court has recognized or protected a relational right of privacy." Harold R. Gordon, the Capone's attorney, countered: "If the court does not intervene, then no one is safe. Any congressman, any senator, any member of the judiciary, and president, upon death becomes fair game for any group of entrepreneurs who decide that they would like to capitalize on his fame and portray him on television for the purpose of selling washing machines, refrigerators, etc." Sonny's attorney also told the court that because of the series his client's children "were ridiculed by their classmates to the extent that they often returned to their home in tears."[288]

The impact of the publicity took its toll on Diana. She divorced Sonny in 1964 and moved to California with the children. This devastated Sonny. He stayed behind in Florida working 16 hours a day at two jobs to support his family. Then, on August 6, 1965, he did something completely out of character; he shoplifted aspirin and flashlight batteries from a North Miami Beach supermarket. Their total worth was $3.50.

Judge Howard S. Klein asked Sonny, "Do you know why you did it?" Sonny, who pleaded no contest, answered, "No, your honor." The judge, noting Sonny's past, placed him on probation for two years.[289] When Sonny's probation was lifted in 1967, his probation officer was told by the tire store manager where Sonny worked that he had been a "steady—and paying—customer."[290]

During this time, Sonny legally changed his name to Albert Francis in a Fort Lauderdale court. Sonny said it was his father's reputation as a Chicago gangster that prompted his decision because it pushed him "into the glare of publicity for even minor violations of the law." Broward County Circuit Judge L. Layton Nance had this response: "The sins of the father are often visited upon the son. I hope you will not besmirch your name so nothing will be visited upon the heads of your children."[291]

In 2011, a file made up of threats against the youngest Kennedy brother, Massachusetts Senator Edward Kennedy, was released by the FBI. It revealed that several weeks after the 1968 assassination of his brother

Robert Kennedy a man from a New England Oyster House in Coral Gables called the Miami FBI office to report that he, his cashier roommate, and a waitress had overheard a man make a threatening phone call against the senator. The man making the threat, who was apparently drunk and identified himself as the son of Al Capone, supposedly said, "If Edward Kennedy keeps fooling around, he's going to get it too." While the FBI confirmed that Sonny was in Miami at the time, no documents revealing a follow up investigation were found.[292]

Sonny moved to Los Altos, California, between San Francisco and San Jose, sometime in the 1980s to be closer to his children. He later moved to Cool, northeast of Sacramento.[293] While in California, he married America "Amie" M. Francis, thirteen years his junior.

Frances Albert "Sonny" Capone who grew up the son of an infamous father and loving and nurturing mother, who tried to live a humble and unobtrusive life filled with the affection of family and friends, died at age 85 on July 8, 2004, in Cool, California.[294]

AFTERWORD

Despite his reputation, or perhaps because of it, the name Al Capone conjures up considerable fascination. During the Prohibition era, his character was larger than life, and he remains, to this day, one of America's most intriguing people.

Al Capone came to Miami to find paradise, in essence, a do-over from his untenable Chicago life and reputation. And while he diligently tried to find perfection by purchasing a beautiful estate, having the grounds customized to fit his every need, enjoying all the amenities the area had to offer, and trying desperately to fit in and stay within the law, still, the lifestyle and peace he truly longed for eluded him. His reputation had preceded him to the Sunshine State, and his taking up residency in Miami Beach only heightened the community's desire to rid itself of any perceived or real threat from his persona or business.

Yes, Al Capone came to Miami in search of paradise, but perhaps what he found was more of a self-imposed prison some might refer to as purgatory.

APPENDIX

93 Palm Avenue

After Capone's death, Mae held on to the house for four more years. In 1952, she sold it to Cleveland realtor Thomas Warren Miller for $64,000. He lived there only a few months then sold it and took with him many of the furnishings Mae had left behind. Most of these furnishings were auctioned off in Chicago in 1992.

The following is a list of the owners of the Capone house after Miller sold it:

- Harry Rendkert - price unknown
- Dr. James C. Chimerakis (Coral Gables physician/surgeon) – price unknown
- 1967 - William Knowles - $48,000
- 1968 - Roy Fowler - $50,000
- 1971 - Henry T. Morrison (Delta airline pilot) - $56,000
- 2011 - Peter Corsell – $5,650,000 - Renovates home.
- 2013 - Eliot 93 – $7,431,750 – Further renovations made.
- 2014 - Carol Invest USA, Inc. – $7,975,000[295]

Architecture and Design

93 Palm Avenue was built in a colonial style with neoclassical details in 1922 and has remained a landmark in Miami Beach for more than 90 years. The 6,103 square foot, two-story main villa is a wood-frame house with stucco and drywall walls.

Entering the house, one encounters a hall with stairs to the upper floor. A living room is situated on one side, a tea room on the other, with the kitchen and dining room in the back. Original features on the main floor include a black-and-gold Art Deco powder room, the 1920's ceiling lights, fireplaces in the living room, and a porch. On the second floor, three of the four bedrooms have their own full bath. Wide verandas with columns and open archways stretch down both sides of the main house.

In the rear of the property, a two-story pool cabana sits on Biscayne Bay. The upper floor is comprised of two mirror-image large rooms, one bedroom and one full bathroom, which are accessed by a spiral staircase.

The gatehouse, which was built during Capone's renovations, is set over one of the entrances and the garage. This structure consists of two double rooms with shared bathroom and one family room with a fireplace.

Next to the gatehouse and opposite the home's entrance is a pond with a little garden bridge, grotto, lighthouse, and waterfall. Each is carved from red coral.

Interesting Facts

• The kitchen had a staircase that Al Capone's black servants used.
• There were once separate bathrooms for men and women at the far end of the family room.
• The property once had a 25 ft. boat dock.
• The pool cabana used to have three diving boards.
• The pool was originally connected to the bay through a grate so the water level would rise and fall. It had salt water, and there were fish and algae.
• The pool was built at 30-by-60-feet to best the Biltmore Hotel's record for largest pool in the area. At Al Capone's time, the pool was the largest private one in Florida.
• The current house maintains its original 93 house number[296]

ENDNOTES

[1] Capone, Deirdre Marie, *Uncle Al Capone*, 2011, p. 188.

[2] Descendants of Vincenzo Capone, Ancestry.com. There is some discrepancy as to when Theresa actually entered the U.S. Some accounts put her entering the country at the same time has her husband Gabrielle. Ancestry.com, however, states that Theresa's second child was born in Italy in 1994. This would indicate that she did not accompany Gabrielle in 1993, but that she came months later, after her second child was born.

[3] Schoenberg, Robert, J., *Mr. Capone, the Real and Complete Story of Al Capone*, 1992, p. 19.

[4] Al Capone, Organized Crime (1899-1947), Biography.com, http://www.biography.com/people/al-capone-9237536#the-crimes. Retrieved September 30, 2015.

[5] Schoenberg, p. 21.

[6] Al Capone, Organized Crime (1899-1947), Biography.com, http://www.biography.com/people/al-capone-9237536#the-crimes.

[7] Schoenberg, pp. 21-24.

[8] Capone, p. 20.

[9] Racketeering is the federal crime of conspiring to organize to commit crimes, especially on an ongoing basis as part of an organized crime operation, U.S. Legal.com. http://www.bing.com/search?q=racketeering&pc=cosp&ptag=A617F1F92B B&form=CONBDF&conlogo=CT3210127

[10] Schoenberg, pp. 29, 31.

[11] "Giacomo "Big Jim" Colosimo – Boss of the Chicago Outfit and Brothel Empire," http://americanmafiahistory.com/giacomo-colosimo/

[12] Ibid, pp. 33-34.

[13] "Capone Dead at 48; Dry Era Gang Chief: Heart Disease at Miami . . .," *New York Times*, January 26, 1947, p. 7.

[14] Schoenberg, p. 35.

[15] "Al Capone," Chicago History, http://chicagohs.org/history/capone/cpn1.html.

[16] "Johnny Torrio;" http://www.imdb.com/name/nm1533252/bio.
[17] Ling, Sally J., *Run the Rum In*, 2007, pp. 20-21.
[18] Schoenberg, 193.
[19] Burnett, Gene, *Florida's Past: People and Events that Shaped the State, Volume 2*, 1996, p. 84.
[20] Ling, p. 38.
[21] ibid, pp. 34, 36.
[22] Ibid, pp. 55-62.
[23] "Al Capone," History, http://www.history.com/topics/al-capone
[24] "Al Capone Biography, Organized Crime 1899-1947," http://www.biography.com/people/al-capone-9237536#the-crimes.
[25] "Johnny Torrio Biography," IMBd, http://www.imdb.com/name/nm1533252/bio.
[26] Schoenberg, p. 123-125.
[27] Deitche, Scott, "Al Capone in St. Petersburg," *Informer*, October 2012, pp. 4-9.
[28] Selected Passenger Lists and Manifests, November 14, 1925, National Archives, Washington, D.C.
[29] Deitche, Scott, "Al Capone in St. Petersburg," *Informer*, October 2012, pp. 4-9.
[30] Ling, p. 42.
[31] "Al Capone," Chicago Historical Society, http://chicagohs.org/history/capone/cpn2a.html. September 30, 2015.
[32] Raab, Selwyn, *Five Families: The Rise, Decline, and Resurgence of America's Most Powerful Mafia Empires*, 2005, p. 42.
[33] Sawyers, June, "Who, Everyone Wanted To Know, Killed McSwiggen?" *Chicago Tribune*, November 27, 1988, http://articles.chicagotribune.com/1988-11-27/features/8802200366_1_al-capone-brew-or-two-beer
[34] Al Capone Biography, Organized Crime 1899-1947, http://www.biography.com/people/al-capone-9237536#the-crimes..
[35] Schoenberg, p. 193.
[36] Press Conference, *Chicago Daily Tribune*, December 6, 1927, p. 1.
[37] Cox, p. 315.
[38] Eller, David, "Historical Essay 5," *Observer*, December 28, 2006.
[39] "Capone is Here as Sun Hunter, He Tells Quigg," *Miami Daily News*, January 10, 1928, pp. 1-2.
[40] Timothy D. Murphy, http://en.wikipedia.org/wiki/Timothy_D._Murphy
[41] "Capone Denies Tim Murphy is Prospective Aid," *Miami Daily News*, January 11, 1928, p. 1.
[42] Eller, David, "Historical Essay 5," *Observer*, December 28, 2006.
[43] Rendering of Sullivan Park by Deerfield Beach Community Redevelopment Agency.
[44] Ling, Sally J., *Run the Rum In*, 2007, p. 102.
[45] Hanley, Robert, "Personal Memoirs," pp. 1-8
[46] Ibid and Mariaurelia, "Smugglers Blues: The Life and Times of Prohibition in Miami," *South Florida*, January 1988, pp. 62, 154.
[47] Ling, p. 43.

[48] Hanley, Robert, "Personal Memoirs," pp. 1-8; Mariaurelia, "Smugglers Blues: The Life and Times of Prohibition in Miami," *South Florida*, January 1988, pp. 62, 154; personal conversation with Stuart Hanley, son of Robert Hanley. Hanley later became a pilot for Pan Am, a Navy pilot and instructor during WWII, owner of his own airline on Catalina Island in California where he flew passengers and cargo for almost two dozen years, and an independent pilot in Jamaica.

[49] Capone, p. 191.

[50] Excerpt taken from Frank Wilson's report on Al Capone's expenditures and trial, Mario Gomes Collection, http://www.myalcaponemuseum.com/id180.htm

[51] Schoenberg, p. 201.

[52] "P.A Henderson Admits Buying Death Pistol," *Miami Daily News*, July 31, 1928, p. 2.

[53] Schoenberg, pp. 194-195.

[54] "P.A Henderson Admits Buying Death Pistol," *Miami Daily News*, July 31, 1928, p. 2.

[55] "Capone's Arsenal Produced Pistol That Killed Yale," *Miami Daily News*, July 31, 1928, pp. 1-2.

[56] Schoenberg, p. 203.

[57] "Capone Announces Retirement as Gang Head; Chicago Doubts," *Miami Daily News*, February 19, 1929, p. 1.

[58] Schoenberg, p. 203.

[59] Ibid, pp. 204-206.

[60] "Florida: The East Coast," *Miami Herald*, 1925.

[61] 1880 United States Census

[62] Dawn McMillan to Sally J. Ling, email, May 5, 2015.

[63] 1910 United States Census

[64] "If You Want to Write, You Can," *The Brooklyn Daily Eagle* (Brooklyn, New York), Sunday, Feb 6, 1927, p. 84.

[65] "Women Plead for Dry Laws," *The Huntsville Daily Times*, March 12, 1930, p. 7, http://www.newspaperabstracts.com/link.php?action=detail&id=75838.

[66] Rosenblum, Constance, *Gold Digger: The Outrageous Life and Times of Peggy Hopkins Joyce*, 2000, p. 85-86.

[67] *The Bankers Magazine*, date unknown, p. 218.

[68] "Statement of Condition of Fidelity Bank and Trust Company," *Illustrated Daily Tab*, p. 30.

[69] Map from Social Index for Palm Beach and Miami Beach, 1940.

[70] "93 Palm Island Background," http://www.93palm.com/#93-palm

[71] 42 Star Island Drive Historical, Preliminary Historical Resources Report, Preservation Board: 7351, February 2013.

[72] "Suit Filed on Capone's Home," *Los Angeles Times*, September 13, 1928, p. 5.

[73] Schoenberg, p. 195.

[74] "Records Show Parker Henderson Took Out Capone House Permits," *Palm Beach Post*, June 23, 1928, p. 1.

[75] Schoenberg, p. 197; "Capone Given Eleven Years Imprisonment," Miami Herald, October 25, 1931, p. 10.

[76] Capone, p. 192.

[77] Kleinberg, Howard, *Miami Beach*, 1994, p. 113; Redford, Polly, *Billion Dollar Sandbar: A Biography of Miami Beach*, 1970, p. 192.

[78] "Demand Mayor quit Features Hectic Session," Miami Daily News, June 27, 1928, pp. 1-2.

[79] Clarence Busch to Governor Doyle E. Carlton, March 25, 1930, Florida State Archives.

[80] Lee Pearson to Sally J. Ling, email, August 20, 2015.

[81] Dawn McMillan to Sally J. Ling, email, May 5, 2015.

[82] "J.B. Orr Body Lies in State until Tuesday," *Miami Daily News*, August 29, 1932, p.1.

[83] Orr, Tom, personal interview, June 5, 2015.

[84] "Capone 'Bodyguard Etiquette' is Discussed by Chief Reeve," *Miami Daily News*, June 23, 1928.

[85] Ling, p. 139.

[86] "Mr. Capone," http://www.mistercapone.com/al_capone_St_Valentines_Day_Massacre.htm

[87] Ling, p. 139.

[88] Schoenberg, p. 223.

[89] Crawford, William G., Jr. "Judge Vincent Giblin, The Life and Times of a South Florida Attorney and Judge." *Tequesta 70*, 2010, p. 68

[90] Schoenberg, p. 221.

[91] "Capone Announces Retirement As Gang Head; Chicago Doubts," *Miami Daily News*, February 18, 1929, p. 1.

[92] Ling, p. 113.

[93] Bousquet, Stephen C., "The Gangster in our Midst: Al Capone in South Florida, 1930-1947, *Florida Historical Quarterly*, 1998, Volume 76 issue 3, p. 307.

[94] Ibid.

[95] Crawford, William G., Jr. "Judge Vincent Giblin, The Life and Times of a South Florida Attorney and Judge." *Tequesta 70*, 2010, p. 69.

[96] Ibid, pp. 68-69.

[97] Capone, p. 153.

[98] Schoenberg, pp. 234, 235, 239.

[99] "Capone Leaves Penitentiary; Dodges Crowd," *Miami Herald*, March 18, 1930, p. 1, 6.

[100] Eastern State Penitentiary, http://www.easternstate.org/support/completed-projects/al-capone-cell-interpretation.

[101] "Capone Leaves Penitentiary; Dodges Crowd," *Miami Herald*, March 18, 1930, p. 1, 6.

[102] Capone, p. 189.

[103] Schoenberg, p. 205.

[104] "Two Brothers of Al Capone are Held Here," *Miami Herald*, March 21, 1930, p. 11.

[105] Schoenberg, p. 254

[106] Ibid.

[107] "Two Brothers of Capone are Held Here," Miami Herald, March 21, 1930, p. 1, 11.

[108] "Capone to Seek U.S. Protection While in Miami," *Miami Daily News*, March 23, 1930, p. 1.

[109] "Chicago Frees Capone When He Surrenders," Miami Herald, March 22, 1930, pp. 1, 3.

[110] "Capone Says Miami Cannot Keep Him Out," *Miami Herald*, March 20, 1930, p. 1.

[111] "Al Capone's Soup Kitchen during the Great Depression," Rare Historical Photos and the Story Behind Them, http://rarehistoricalphotos.com/al-capones-soup-kitchen-great-depression-chicago-1931/.

[112] "Oust Capone, Carlton Orders Sheriffs, Miami Daily News, March 19, 1930, p. 1.

[113] Bousquet, Stephen C., "The Gangster in Our Midst: Al Capone in South Florida, 1930-1947," *Florida Historical Quarterly*, Volume 76 Issue 3, 1998, p. 302.

[114] *Time*: The Weekly Magazine, Volume XV, Number 12.

[115] Bousquet, Stephen C., "The Gangster in Our Midst: Al Capone in South Florida, 1930-1947," *Florida Historical Quarterly*, Volume 76 Issue 3, 1998, p. 300.

[116] Capone, p. 190.

[117] "New Ban on Capone Declared in Florida," New York Times, March 25, 1930, p. 5.

[118] Crawford, William G., Jr., "Judge Vincent Giblin, The Life and Times of a South Florida Attorney and Judge," *Tequesta 70*, 2010, p. 69.

[119] "Gunman Threat Sent Sheriff at Lauderdale," *Miami Daily News*, March 20, 1930, pp. 1-2.

[120] Joel Johnston to Governor Carlton, March 25, 1930, Florida State Archives.

[121] H. Marsh to Governor Doyle e. Carlton, March 25, 1930, Florida State Archives.

[122] Angus Sumner to Hon. Doyle E. Carlton, March 27, 1930, Florida State Archives.

[123] Otto M. Schauberger to Governor Carlton, March 27, 1930, Florida State Archives.

[124] Clarence E. Woods to Judge Frank A. Katzentine, April 17, 1930, Florida State Archives.

[125] Crawford, William G., Jr., "Judge Vincent Giblin, The Life and Times of a South Florida Attorney and Judge," *Tequesta 70*, 2010, pp. 59-65.

[126] Ibid, p. 70.

[127] "Capone Free to Enter Florida without Fear of Molestation," *Gettysburg Times*, March 25, 1930, p.5.

[128] Crawford, William G., Jr., "Judge Vincent Giblin, The Life and Times of a South Florida Attorney and Judge," *Tequesta 70*, 2010, p. 70.

[129] Schoenberg, p. 223.

[130] Some accounts note Tony was McGurn's half-brother.

[131] "McGurn Aids Drop Effort to Liberate Gangster Here," *Miami Daily News*, April 1, 1930, pp. 1, 10. While the Miami Daily News referred to Tony as Jack

McGurn's brother, other references state he was Tony Demory, McGurn's half-brother. Capone, p. 356.

[132] "'Machine Gun' Jack McGurn," The Outlaw Journals, http://www.babyfacenelsonjournal.com/jack-mcgurn.html

[133] "Al Capone Slips Into Home Here as Thousands at Easter Service," *Miami Daily News*, April 21, 1930, p. 1.

[134] "Capone Announces Retirement as Gang Head; Chicago Doubts," *Miami Daily News*, February 18, 1929, p. 1-2.

[135] "History of *The Miami News* (1886-1987), *Tequesta*, Number XLVII (1987), pp. 23, 24.

[136] Cox, pp. 315-316.

[137] Kleinberg, Howard, *Miami Beach*, Centennial Press, 1994, p. 116.

[138] Bousquet, Stephen C., "The Gangster in Our Midst: Al Capone in South Florida, 1930-1947," *Florida Historical Quarterly*, Volume 76 Issue 3, 1998, p. 302.

[139] Redford, Polly, "*Million Dollar Sandbar: A Biography of Miami Beach*," pp. 195-196, 198.

[140] Kleinberg, p. 116.

[141] Cox, p. 315.

[142] Redford, p. 195.

[143] "Al Capone Slips Into Home Here As Thousands at Easter Service," *Miami Daily News*, April 21, 1930, p. 1.

[144] Capone, p. 188.

[145] Crawford, William G., Jr., "Judge Vincent Giblin, The Life and Times of a South Florida Attorney and Judge," *Tequesta 70*, 2010, p. 73.

[146] Carlton, Doyle E., Press Release, State of Florida, Executive Department, Florida State Archives.

[147] Crawford, William G., Jr., "Judge Vincent Giblin, The Life and Times of a South Florida Attorney and Judge," *Tequesta 70*, 2010, p. 73-74.

[148] "Al Capone is Called before Cuban Chief of Secret Service," *Miami Daily News*, April 30, 1930, p. 1.

[149] "Capone Ready to Defend Home," *Miami Daily News*, May 1, 1930, p. 1.

[150] "Capone Hearing Date to be Set by Court Today," *Miami Daily News*, May 13, 1930, p. 1.

[151] "Capone Trip to Havana May Be Troublesome," *Miami Daily News*, March 28, 1930, pp. 1-2.

[152] Schoenberg, p. 266.

[153] "25 Capone Henchmen Indicted by Federal Jury in Rum Probe," *Miami Daily News*, May 1, 1930, p. 1.

[154] "How Capone's Gang Escaped Rivals While Golfing Is Told," *Miami Daily News*, April 3, 1930, pp. 1, 15.

[155] "Jersey Mayor Mistaken for Capone on Steamer Trip from Cuba," *Miami Daily News*, May 7, 1930, p. 1.

[156] "Capone's Demurrer in Padlocking Case Studied by Jurist," *Miami Daily News*, April 26, 1930, p. 1.

[157] "Grebstein's Answer Admits Fund Confab with Miami Jurist," *Miami Daily News*, May 26, 1930, p. 1.

[158] Crawford, William G., Jr., "Judge Vincent Giblin, The Life and Times of a South Florida Attorney and Judge," *Tequesta 70*, 2010, p. 76.

[159] Many books on Capone note this movie as "The Adventures of Fu Manchu." This movie, however, was not released until 1956.

[160] Crawford, William G., Jr., "Judge Vincent Giblin, The Life and Times of a South Florida Attorney and Judge," *Tequesta 70*, 2010, p. 74

[161] Schoenberg, p. 267.

[162] "Capone Seeks U.S. Court Order Against Police; Wharton Given Warning to Leave After Attack," *Miami Daily News*, May 9, 1930, p. 1.

[163] Ibid.

[164] Schoenberg, p. 268; "Case of Capone and 3 Pals Set for Afternoon," *Miami Daily News*, May 15, 1930, p. 1-2.

[165] "Capone-Owned Clubs Raided by U.S. Agents," *Miami Daily News*, May 8, 1930, p. 1.

[166] "$75,000 Worth of Capone Rum is Confiscated," *Miami Daily News*, May 13, 1930, p.1.

[167] Schoenberg, p. 269.

[168] Crawford, William G., Jr., "Judge Vincent Giblin, The Life and Times of a South Florida Attorney and Judge," *Tequesta 70*, 2010, p. 76.

[169] "Capone and Aid Freed by Judge in City Court," *Miami Daily News*, May 21, 1930, p. 1.

[170] Al Capone Quotes, http://www.great-quotes.com/quotes/author/Al/Capone

[171] "Capone Escapes Arrest by Call on his Lawyer," *Miami Daily News*, May 24, 1930, p. 1.

[172] Schoenberg, p. 270.

[173] "Fisher Testifies that Capone Presence makes Beach Citizens Fearful, Cuts Property Values," *Miami Daily News*, May 16, 1930, pp. 1, 4.

[174] Redford, P. 194.

[175] "Capone Attorneys Rebuked by Judge at Padlock Trial," *Miami Daily News*, June 6, 1930, p. 1.

[176] Crawford, William G., Jr., "Judge Vincent Giblin, The Life and Times of a South Florida Attorney and Judge," *Tequesta 70*, 2010, p. 78.

[177] "Rum Order for Pine at Home of Capone is Told by Witness," *Miami Daily News*, June 11, 1930, pp. 1, 10.

[178] Redford, p. 194; Crawford, William G., Jr., "Judge Vincent Giblin, The Life and Times of a South Florida Attorney and Judge," *Tequesta 70*, 2010, p. 78.

[179] Crawford, William G., Jr., "Judge Vincent Giblin, The Life and Times of a South Florida Attorney and Judge," *Tequesta 70*, 2010, p. 79.

[180] Ibid.

[181] Community Chest was a philanthropic organization (1913-1963) that became the United Way.

[182] Crawford, William G., Jr., "Judge Vincent Giblin, The Life and Times of a South Florida Attorney and Judge," *Tequesta 70*, 2010, p. 79.

[183] Redford, p. 193.

[184] Ibid. 193.

[185] Schoenberg, p. 271.

[186] "Capone Plans First of Good Will Dinners," Miami Daily News, May 27, 1930, p. 1.

[187] Ibid; Kleinberg, p. 115.

[188] Schoenberg, p. 271.

[189] Ibid.

[190] "Capone Arrested on Perjury Charge," *Miami Daily News*, June 14, 1930, p.1, 10.

[191] Ibid.

[192] Schoenberg, p. 273.

[193] "Capone Arrested on Perjury Charge," *Miami Daily News*, June 14, 1930, p. 1.

[194] "Newcomb Rules M'Creary Case to be Reopened," *Miami Daily News*, June 19, 1930, p. 1.

[195] Crawford, William G., Jr., "Judge Vincent Giblin, The Life and Times of a South Florida Attorney and Judge," *Tequesta 70*, 2010, p. 82.

[196] Schoenberg, p. 273.

[197] "Pine's Denial Branded 'Lie' by Tub Palmer," Miami Daily News, June 21, 1930, p. 1, 10.

[198] "Death Writes End to Charmed Life of Fred Pine, 63," *Miami Herald*, February 26, 1966.

[199] Capone, p. 189.

[200] Crawford, William G., Jr., "Judge Vincent Giblin, The Life and Times of a South Florida Attorney and Judge," *Tequesta 70*, 2010, p. 83.

[201] Ibid.

[202] "Capone Seeks Foothold in Broward," *Fort Lauderdale Daily News*, July 2, 1930, p.1.

[203] "Capone's Attorney buys Tract of Land," *Palm Beach Post*, July 3, 1930, p.1.

[204] "Miami Ending Drive Against Al Capone; Charges Dropped," *Palm Beach Post*, July 16, 1930, p. 1.

[205] McDougald Shadoin, Margaret, Oral interview with Author, 2006.

[206] "Work to Start Soon on New Capone Home," Palm Beach Post, July 15, 1930, p. 1.

[207] Crawford, William G., Jr., "Capone Island: From Swampland to Broward County's Deerfield Island Park, 150 Years of Florida Land History," *Broward Legacy*, Vol. 19 no 3-4, 1996, pp. 22-24.

[208] Eller, David, "Historical Essay 5," *Observer*, December 28, 2006.

[209] Capone, pp. 78-79.

[210] Ibid, p. 189.

[211] Schoenberg, pp. 304-305.

[212] "Beach Clamps Lid on Crime at Fiery Meet," Miami Daily News, January 14, 1931, p. 1, 7.

[213] "Let's Keep Gambling Out," Miami Herald, August 4, 1931, p. 1.

[214] "Beach Clamps Lid on Crime at Fiery Meet," Miami Daily News, January 14, 1931, p. 1, 7.

[215] Carol Orr Hartman in email to Sally J. Ling, May 21, 2015.

[216] "Mayor Jack Orr Dies," Miami Daily News, July 15, 1974, p. 7A.

[217] "John B. Orr, An Appreciation," Dade County's Civic Digest, August 30, 1932.

[218] "John B. Orr," A Book of the South," 1940, pp. 133, 144; J.B. Orr Body Lies in State Until Tuesday, Miami Daily News, August 29, 1932, pp. 1-2.

[219] "J.B. Orr Body Lies in State until Tuesday," Miami Daily News, August 29, 1932, p. 2.

[220] Letter dated July 8, 1931, from W.C. Hodgins, Jacque L. Westrich, and H.N. Clagett, all Internal Revenue Agents, to the Internal Revenue Agent in Charge, Chicago, Illinois, in re Alphonse Capone, 7244 Prairie Avenue, Chicago, Illinois, http://www.irs.gov/pub/irs-utl/file-1-letter-dated-07081931-in-re-alphonse-capone.pdf. Retrieved September 30, 2015.

[221] Ibid, pp. 298-300.

[222] "Capone Given Eleven Years Imprisonment," Miami Herald, October 15, 1931, p. 10.

[223] Schoenberg, p. 324.

[224] "Capone Given Eleven Years Imprisonment," Miami Herald, October 15, 1931, p. 10.

[225] Schoenberg, p. 311.

[226] "Ex-Judge Giblin Fiery Champ," Miami Daily News, March 21, 1965, p. 3; "Vincent Giblin, Ex-Judge, Dies; Had Been Lawyer for Capone," New York Times, March 22, 1965, p. 33.

[227] Crawford, William G., Jr., "Judge Vincent Giblin, The Life and Times of a South Florida Attorney and Judge," Tequesta 70, 2010, p. 88; Schoenberg, pp. 311-312.

[228] Crawford, William G., Jr., "Judge Vincent Giblin, The Life and Times of a South Florida Attorney and Judge," Tequesta 70, 2010, p. 85, 88.

[229] Schoenberg, pp. 324-325.

[230] "Capone Given Eleven Years Imprisonment," Miami Herald, October 25, 1931, p. 1.

[231] Schoenberg, pp. 335-337.

[232] "Capone is Broke, Miami Estate is his Only Asset," Palm Beach Daily News, December 22, 1938, p. 1.

[233] Schoenberg, pp. 349-350.

[234] "Capone is Broke, Miami Estate is his Only Asset," Palm Beach Daily News, December 22, 1938, p. 1.

[235] Schoenberg, p. 342.

[236] Wasserman Test, https://en.wikipedia.org/wiki/Wassermann_test.

[237] Schoenberg, pp. 343, 345.

[238] Al Capone," History Files, Chicago Historical Society,
http://chicagohs.org/history/capone/cpn4.html.

[239] Capone, p. 73.

[240] "Al Capone," History Files, Chicago Historical Society,
http://chicagohs.org/history/capone/cpn4.html.

[241] Schoenberg, pp. 347-349.

[242] Capone, p. 191.

[243] "Al Capone Auction Documents Reveals Dementia, Violent Outbursts,"
http://www.huffingtonpost.com/2013/05/31/al-capone-auction_n_3367770.html.

[244] "History of Penicillin,"
http://inventors.about.com/od/pstartinventions/a/Penicillin.htm.

[245] Schoenberg, p. 352.

[246] Crawford, William G., Jr., "Judge Vincent Giblin, The Life and Times of a South Florida Attorney and Judge," *Tequesta 70*, 2010, p. 92.

[247] Schoenberg, p. 352.

[248] "Oxygen Tent Used in Prolonging Dying Capone's Life," *Miami Daily News*, January 25, 1947, pp. 1-2.

[249] Ex-Gang Overlord Clings to Life in Guarded Palm Island Home," *Miami Daily News*, January 22, 1947, p. 1.

[250] Capone, p. 115-116

[251] Ibid.

[252] Al Capone Medical report, http://www.huffingtonpost.com/2013/05/31/al-capone-auction_n_3367770.html.

[253] Capone, p. 117.

[254] Ibid.

[255] "Oxygen Tent Used in Prolonging Dying Capone's Life," *Miami Daily News*, January 25, 1947, pp. 1-2.

[256] Capone, p. 354.

[257] "Capone Reported Now Out of Danger," Miami Daily News, January 23, 1947, p. 1.

[258] Capone, p. 117.

[259] Capone, p. 120.

[260] Al Capone Medical report, http://www.huffingtonpost.com/2013/05/31/al-capone-auction_n_3367770.html

[261] "Oxygen Tent Used in Prolonging Dying Capone's Life," *Miami Daily News*, January 25, 1947, pp. 1-2.

[262] Capone, p. 120.

[263] "Brother Won't Talk of Capone Funeral," Miami Daily News, January 27, 1947, p. 1.

[264] Capone, p. 120.

[265] "Al Capone," http://chicagohs.org/history/capone/cpn4.html.

[266] "Al Capone, Let Us Blush," Miami Daily News, January 26, 1947, p. 8B.

[267] Schoenberg, pp. 292, 360.

[268] Descendants of Vincenzo Capone, Ancestry.com

[269] Capone, p. 188.

[270] Syphilis – Cause, WebMD.com, http://www.webmd.com/sexual-conditions/tc/syphilis-cause

[271] Kleinberg, Eliot, "He Was Capone's Son," *South Florida History*, Volume 36, No. 2 (2008), p. 13.

[272] Ibid.

[273] Capone, p. 148.

[274] Desi Arnaz, Bio., http://www.biography.com/people/desi-arnaz-9542545

[275] Carol Orr Hartman, email and oral interview with author, May 21, 2015.

[276] Capone, p. 63.

[277] Schoenberg, p. 251; Janesblogspot.com.

[278] Schoenberg, pp. 351-352.

[279] Descendants of Albert Francis "Sonny" Capone, Ancestry.com

[280] "Capone Takes Bride," *Reno Evening Gazette*, January 2, 1941, p. 12.

[281] Descendants of Albert Francis "Sonny" Capone, Ancestry.com

[282] Gomes, Mario, myalcaponemuseum.com

[283] Schoenberg, p. 362.

[284] "The Untouchables" (1959-1963 TV Series), https://books.google.com/books?id=2DYOlx4_Qk4C&pg=PA47&lpg=PA47&dq=The+Untouchables+could+not+be+bribed+or+intimidated+by+the+Mob.&source=bl&ots=_XQXctDAS2&sig=SFLWgQZ6SOj2jV1hhKsNqwfTMcE&hl=en&sa=X&ei=5WydUsLmB4_aoASbmYKQBw&ved=0CCoQ6AEwAA#v=onepage&q=The%20Untouchables%20could%20not%20be%20bribed%20or%20intimidated%20by%20the%20Mob.&f=false.

[285] Desi Arnaz, "Desi Arnaz & Lucille Ball: The Geniuses Who Shaped The Future Of Television". Entrepreneur. October 8, 2009. Retrieved September 30, 2015. http://www.entrepreneur.com/article/197550

[286] Ibid.

[287] Schoenberg, p. 352.

[288] "Capones Lose Privacy Appeal," *Corpus Christi Times*, October 19, 1965, p. 1.

[289] "Son of Scarface Al' in Court on a Piddling $3.40 Shoplift," *Press Telegram* (Long Beach, California), November 16, 1965, p. 1.

[290] Kleinberg, Eliot, "He Was Capone's Son," *South Florida History*, Volume 36, No. 2 (2008), p. 13.

[291] "Al Capone, Jr., Changes Name,"*Humbodt Standard* (Eureka, California), May 10, 1966, p. 1.

[292] Bender, Bryan and Levenson, Michael, " FBI Files Show Decades of Threats against Kennedy," *The Boston Globe*, August 2, 2011. http://www.boston.com/news/nation/washington/articles/2011/08/02/fbi_files_detail_decades_of_threats_against_edward_kennedy/

[293] Kleinberg, Eliot, "He Was Capone's Son," *South Florida History*, Volume 36, No. 2 (2008), p. 13.
[294] "Descendants of Albert Francis 'Sonny' Capone," Ancestry.com.
[295] Miami Dade County Property Appraiser website, http://www.miamidade.gov/propertysearch/#/
[296] 93 Palm website, http://www.93palm.com/facts-figures

BIBLIOGRAPHY

Books

A Book of the South. "John B. Orr." The Jas. O. Jones Company, 1940.

Burnett, Gene. *Florida's Past: People and Events that Shaped the State*, Volume 2. Pineapple Press, 1996.

Capone, Deirdre Marie. *Uncle Al Capone.* Recap Publishing Company, 2011.

Cox, James M. *Journey through My Years.* Simon and Schuster, 1946.

Kleinberg, Howard. *Miami Beach.* Centennial Press, 1994.

Klepser, Carolyn. *Lost Miami Beach.* The History Press, 2014.

Ling, Sally J. *Run the Rum In.* The History Press, 2007.

Raab, Selwyn. *Five Families: The Rise, Decline, and Resurgence of America's Most Powerful Mafia Empires.* Thomas Dunne Books/St. Martin's Press, 2006.

Redford, Polly. *Billion Dollar Sandbar: A Biography of Miami Beach.* Clarke, Irwin & Company Limited, 1970.

Rosenblum, Constance. Gold Digger: *The Outrageous Life and Times of Peggy Hopkins Joyce.* Henry Holt and Co., 2000.

Schoenberg, Robert J. *Mr. Capone: The Real and Complete Story of Al Capone.* William Morrow & Company, Inc. 1993.

Van de Water, Frederick F. *The Real McCoy.* Flat Hammock Press, 2007. First published 1931 by Doubleday Doran.

Newspapers and Periodicals

"25 Capone Henchmen Indicted by Federal Jury in Rum Probe." *Miami Daily News.* May 1, 1930.

"$75,000 Worth of Capone Rum is Confiscated." *Miami Daily News*, May 13, 1930.

"FBI files show decades of threats against Kennedy." *The Boston Globe*. Bender, Bryan and Levenson, Michael, August 2, 2011.

"Al Capone is Called before Cuban Chief of Secret Service." *Miami Daily News*, April 30, 1930.

"Al Capone, Jr., Changes Name."*Humbodt Standard* (Eureka, California), May 10, 1966.

"Al Capone, Let Us Blush." Miami Daily News, January 26, 1947.

"Al Capone Slips Into Home Here as Thousands at Easter Service." *Miami Daily News*, April 21, 1930.

Bankers Magazine, date unknown.

"Beach Clamps Lid on Crime at Fiery Meet." Miami Daily News, January 14, 1931.

Bousquet, Stephen. "The Gangster in our Midst: Al Capone in South Florida, 1930-1947." *Florida Historical Quarterly*, Volume 76, Issue 3 (1998).

"Brother Won't Talk of Capone Funeral." Miami Daily News, January 27, 1947.

"Capone and Aid Freed by Judge in City Court." *Miami Daily News*, May 21, 1930.

"Capone Announces Retirement as Gang Head; Chicago Doubts." *Miami Daily News*, February 19, 1929.

"Capone Arrested on Perjury Charge." *Miami Daily News*, June 14, 1930.

"Capone Attorneys Rebuked by Judge at Padlock Trial." *Miami Daily News*, June 6, 1930.

"Capone's Arsenal Produced Pistol That Killed Yale." *Miami Daily News*, July 31, 1928.

"Capone 'Bodyguard Etiquette' is Discussed by Chief Reeve." *Miami Daily News*, June 23, 1928.

"Capone Dead at 48; Dry Era Gang Chief: Heart Disease at Miami . . ." *New York Times*, January 26, 1947.

"Capone Denies Tim Murphy is Prospective Aid." *Miami Daily News*, January 11, 1928.

"Capone Escapes Arrest by Call on his Laywer." *Miami Daily News*, May 24, 1930.

"Capone Free to Enter Florida without Fear of Molestation." *Gettysburg Times*, March 25, 1930.

"Capone Given Eleven Years Imprisonment." Miami Herald, October 25, 1931.

"Capone Hearing Date to be Set by Court Today." *Miami Daily News*, May 13, 1930.

"Capone is Broke, Miami Estate is his Only Asset." Palm Beach Daily News, December 22, 1938.

"Capone is Here as Sun Hunter, He Tells Quigg." *Miami Daily News*, January 10, 1928.

"Capone Leaves Penitentiary; Dodges Crowd." *Miami Herald*, March 18, 1930.

"Capone-Owned Clubs Raided by U.S. Agents." *Miami Daily News*, May 8, 1930.

"Capone Ready to Defend Home." *Miami Daily News*, May 1, 1930.

"Capone Says Miami Cannot Keep Him Out." *Miami Herald*, March 20, 1930.

"Capone Takes Bride." *Reno Evening Gazette*. January 2, 1941.

"Capone to Seek U.S. Protection While in Miami." *Miami Daily News*, March 23, 1930.

"Capone Trip to Havana May Be Troublesome." *Miami Daily News*, March 28, 1930.

"Capone given Eleven Years Imprisonment." *Miami Herald*, October 15, 1931.

"Capone Plans First of Good Will Dinners." Miami Daily News, May 27, 1930.

"Capone Reported Now Out of Danger." Miami Daily News, January 23, 1947.

"Capone Seeks Foothold in Broward." *Fort Lauderdale Daily News*, July 2, 1930.

"Capone Seeks U.S. Court Order Against Police; Wharton Given Warning to Leave After Attack*." Miami Daily News*, May 9, 1920.

"Capones Lose Privacy Appeal." *Corpus Christi Times*, October 19, 1965.

"Capone's Attorney buys Tract of Land." *Palm Beach Post*, July 3, 1930.

"Capone's Demurrer in Padlocking Case Studied by Jurist." *Miami Daily News*, April 26, 1930.

"Chicago Frees Capone When He Surrenders." Miami Herald, March 22, 1930.

Crawford, William G., Jr. "Judge Vincent Giblin, The Life and Times of a South Florida Attorney and Judge." *Tequesta 70* 2010.

------- "The Town of Boca Raton and the Capone Tract." *Broward Legacy* 19, nos. 3-4 (Summer/Fall 1996).

"Demand May Quit Features Hectic Session." *Miami Daily News*, June 27, 1928.

Deitche, Scott. *"Al Capone in St. Petersburg."* *Informer*, October 2012.

Eller, David, "Historical Essay 5." *Observer*, December 28, 2006.

"Ex-Gang Overlord Clings to Life in Guarded Palm Island Home." *Miami Daily News*, January 22, 1947.

"Ex-Judge Giblin Fiery Champ." *Miami Daily News*, March 21, 1965.

"Fisher Testifies that Capone Presence makes Beach Citizens Fearful, Cuts Property Values." *Miami Daily News*, May 16, 1930.

"Florida: The East Coast." *Miami Herald*, 1925.

"Gunman Threat Sent Sheriff at Lauderdale." *Miami Daily News*, March 20, 1930.

"Grebstein's Answer Admits Fund Confab with Miami Jurist." *Miami Daily News*, May 26, 1930.

"How Capone's Gang Escaped Rivals While Golfing Is Told." *Miami Daily News*, April 3, 1930.

"If You Want to Write, You Can." *The Brooklyn Daily Eagle* (Brooklyn, New York), Sunday, Feb 6, 1927.

"J.B. Orr Body Lies in State until Tuesday." *Miami Daily News*, August 29, 1932.

"Jersey Mayor Mistaken for Capone on Steamer Trip from Cuba." *Miami Daily News*, May 7, 1930.

Kleinberg, Eliot. "He was Capone's Son." *South Florida History*, Volume 36, No 2 (2008).

"Let's Keep Gambling Out." Miami Herald, August 4, 1931.

"Mayor Jack Orr Dies." *Miami Daily News*, July 15, 1974.

"McGurn Aids Drop Effort to Liberate Gangster Here." *Miami Daily News*, April 1, 1930.

"Miami Ending Drive Against Al Capone; Charges Dropped." *Palm Beach Post*, July 16, 1930.

"New Ban on Capone Declared in Florida." New York Times, March 25, 1930.

"Newcomb Rules McCreary Case to be Reopened." *Miami Daily News*, June 19, 1930.

"Oust Capone, Carlton Orders Sheriffs, Miami Daily News, March 19, 1930.

"Oxygen Tent Used in Prolonging Dying Capone's Life." *Miami Daily News*, January 25, 1947.

"P.A Henderson Admits Buying Death Pistol." *Miami Daily News*, July 31, 1928.

"Pine's Denial Branded 'Lie' by Tub Palmer." Miami Daily News, June 21, 1930.

"Records Show Parker Henderson Took Out Capone House Permits." *Palm Beach Post*, June 23, 1928.

"Rum Order for Pine at Home of Capone is Told by Witness." *Miami Daily News*, June 11, 1930.

"Son of Scarface Al' in Court on a Piddling $3.40 Shoplift." *Press Telegram* (Long Beach, California), November 16, 1965.

Sterns Realty Service. "Palm and Hibiscus Islands." Florida: The East Coast. *Miami Herald*, 1925.

Sorensen, Eve. "If You Want to Write, You Can." *The Brooklyn Daily Eagle* (Brooklyn, New York), Sunday, Feb 6, 1927.

"Suit Filed on Capone's Home." *Los Angeles Times*, September 13, 1928.

"Two Brothers of Al Capone are Held Here." *Miami Herald*, March 21, 19301.

"Vincent Giblin, Ex-Judge, Dies, Had Been Lawyer for Capone." *New York Times*, March 22, 1965.

"Who, Everyone Wanted To Know, Killed McSwiggen?" Sawyers, June. *Chicago Tribune*, November 27, 1988.

"Women Plead for Dry Laws." *The Huntsville Daily Times*, March 12, 1930.

"Work to Start Soon on New Capone Home." Palm Beach Post, July 15, 1930.

Documents

Busch, Clarence M. Letter to Governor Doyle E. Carlton. March 25, 1930. Florida State Archives

Carlton, Doyle E., Press Release, State of Florida, Executive Department, Florida State Archives.

Garnto, A. M. Letter to Governor Doyle E. Carlton, July 16, 1930. Florida State Archives.

Hanley, Robert, Personal Memoirs.

Johnston, Joel. Letter to Governor Doyle E. Carlton, March 25, 1930. Florida State Archives.

Marsh, H. Letter to Fovernor Doyle E. Carlton, March 25, 1930. Florida State Archives.

Schauberger, Otto, M. Letter to Governor Doyle E. Carlton, March 27, 1930. Florida State Archives.

Woods, Clarence E. Letter to Governor Doyle E. Carlton, April 17, 1930. Florida State Archives.

Press Release, Governor Doyle E. Carlton, 1930. Florida State Archives.

Florida Passenger Lists 1898-1951 (Provo, UT, USA, Ancestry.com Operations Inc, 2006), Ancestry.com, Record for Alphonse Capone. http://search.ancestry.com/cgi-bin/sse.dll?db=flpl&h=3304519&indiv=try.

Capone Indictment. U.S. National Archives.

Maps/Images

"Miami Beach off Causeway, Palm and Hibiscus Islands." <u>Social Index</u> for Palm Beach and Miami Beach, 1940.

Rendering of Sullivan Park by Deerfield Beach Community Redevelopment Agency. City of Deerfield Beach.

Personal Interviews

Hanley, Stuart. September 23, 2015.

Hartman, Carol Orr. May 21, 2015.

Hartman, Tom. June 5, 2015.

McMillan, Dawn. May 5, 2015

Pearson, Reverend Lee. August 20, 2015.

Websites

While the author made every attempt to accurately document the websites used in this work, websites change and evolve over time. Because of this, the author cannot vouch for the accuracy of the websites at the time of publication.

"93 Palm Island Backgrounder." http://www.93palm.com/#93-palm.

Al Capone Quotes. http://www.great-quotes.com/quotes/author/Al/Capone

Albert Frances "Sonny" Capone. Findagrave.com http://www.findagrave.com/cgi-bin/fg.cgi?page=gr&GRid=77124965.

"Al Capone Auction Documents Reveals Dementia, Violent Outbursts." http://www.huffingtonpost.com/2013/05/31/al-capone-auction_n_3367770.html.

"Al Capone," Chicago History, http://chicagohs.org/history/capone/cpn1.html.

Al Capone Medical report. http://www.huffingtonpost.com/2013/05/31/al-capone-auction_n_3367770.html.

"Al Capone." WPBT2, People & Events. http://www.pbs.org/wgbh/amex/miami/peopleevents/pande01.html.

"Al Capone, Organized Crime (1899-1947)." Biography. http://www.biography.com/people/al-capone-9237536#the-crimes.

Bender, Bryan and Levenson, Michael. " FBI files show decades of threats against Kennedy." *The Boston Globe*, August 2, 2011.

http://www.boston.com/news/nation/washington/articles/2011/08/02/fbi_files_detail_decades_of_threats_against_edward_kennedy/

"Descendants of Albert Francis 'Sonny' Capone." Ancestry.com.

"Desi Arnaz & Lucille Ball: The Geniuses Who Shaped The future of Television." Entrepreneur. October 8, 2009. http://www.entrepreneur.com/article/197550

"Fulgencio Batista." Fulgencio Batista, http://www.britannica.com/biography/Fulgencio-Batista

Gomes, Mario, myalcaponemuseum.com.

"History of Penicillin." http://inventors.about.com/od/pstartinventions/a/Penicillin.htm.

"Jake Guzik." https://en.wikipedia.org/wiki/Jake_Guzik.

"Johnny Torrio Biography." http://www.imdb.com/name/nm1533252/bio.

myalcaponemuseum.com.

Letter dated July 8, 1931, from W.C. Hodgins, Jacque L. Westrich, and H.N. Clagett, all Internal Revenue Agents, to the Internal Revenue Agent in Charge, Chicago, Illinois, in re Alphonse Capone, 7244 Prairie Avenue, Chicago, Illinois. http://www.irs.gov/pub/irs-utl/file-1-letter-dated-07081931-in-re-alphonse-capone.pdf.

"'Machine Gun' Jack McGurn," The Outlaw Journals, http://www.babyfacenelsonjournal.com/jack-mcgurn.html

Piket, Casey. "Al Capone in Miami." Miami Museum of History, http://miami-history.com/al-capone-in-miami.

Sawyers, June. "Who, Everyone Wanted To Know, Killed McSwiggen?" *Chicago Tribune*, November 27, 1988. http://articles.chicagotribune.com/1988-11-27/features/8802200366_1_al-capone-brew-or-two-beer

"The Untouchables" (1959-1963 TV Series). http://en.wikipedia.org/wiki/The_Untouchables_(1959-63_TV_series).

Excerpt taken from Frank Wilson's report on Al Capone's expenditures and trial, Mario Gomes Collection. http://www.myalcaponemuseum.com/id180.htm.

Wasserman Test. https://en.wikipedia.org/wiki/Wassermann_test.

INDEX

ABOUT THE AUTHOR

Sally J. Ling, Florida's History Detective, is an author, speaker and historian. She writes historical fiction and nonfiction and specializes in little known stories of Florida history.

As a special correspondent, Sally wrote for the *Sun Sentinel* newspaper for four years and has been a contributing journalist for *Boca Raton, Gold Coast, Delray Beach, Boca Life, Jupiter Palm Beacher, and Lighthouse Point* magazines.

Based upon excerpts from her book *Run the Rum In,* Sally appeared in two TV documentaries ("Gangsters" - the National Geographic Channel, and "Prohibition and the South Florida Connection" - WLRN, Miami). She served as associate producer on the latter production. In addition, her book *Who Killed Leno and Louise?* was made into a mini-documentary by WLRN. It won an Emmy at the 2015 Sun Coast Chapter awards presentation. The station is currently in production on a feature length WWII documentary based upon her book *Small Town, Big Secrets.*

Sally has been a guest on South Florida PBS TV and radio stations, guest presenter at the Lifelong Learning Society at Florida Atlantic University and Future Authors of America, and guest speaker at numerous historical societies, libraries, organizations, and schools.

She lives with her husband, Chuck, and splits her time between South Florida, and western North Carolina.

Contact Sally at info@sallyjling.com

Sally's books include:

Nonfiction

- *Al Capone's Miami: Paradise or Purgatory?*
- *Out of Mind, Out of Sight: A Revealing History of the Florida State Hospital at Chattahoochee and Mental Health Care in Florida*
- *Sailin' on the Stranahan*
- *Run the Rum In: South Florida during Prohibition*
- *Small Town, Big Secrets: Inside the Boca Raton Army Airfield during World War II (First and Second editions)*
- *A History of Boca Raton*
- *Fund Raising With Golf*

Fiction

- *Who Killed Leno and Louise?*
- *The Spear of Destiny: A Shea Baker Mystery (Volume 2)*
- *The Cloak: A Shea Baker Mystery (Volume 1)*
- *The Tree and the Carpenter*
- *Spies, Root Beer and Alligators: Phillip's Great Adventures*

You may contact Sally at: info@sallyjling.com

For information on Sally's current projects, or to become a *"Preferred Reader,"* please visit her website at: sallyjling.com.

CPSIA information can be obtained at www.ICGtesting.com
Printed in the USA
LVOW10s1801070416

482606LV00021B/1209/P

9 780996 433310